PROJECT PEACEMAKERS
745 WESTMINSTER AVE.
WINNIPEG, MANITOBA
R3G 1A5 (204) 775-8178

PEACE, WAR & YOUTH

Books in the YOUTH WORLD Series

PEACE, WAR & YOUTH
CONTEMPORARY FILM
 & THE NEW GENERATION
POPULAR SONG & YOUTH TODAY

PEACE, WAR & YOUTH

EDITED BY

LOUIS M. SAVARY

MAUREEN P. COLLINS

PHOTOGRAPHS BY

SHELLY RUSTEN

This piecemeal peace is no peace.
Gerard Manley Hopkins

ASSOCIATION PRESS
NEW YORK

PEACE, WAR & YOUTH
Copyright © 1971 by Association Press
291 Broadway, New York, N. Y. 10007

All rights reserved. No part of this publication may be reprinted, reproduced, transmitted, stored in a retrieval system, or otherwise utilized, in any form or by any means, electronic or mechanical, including photocopying or recording, now existing or hereinafter invented, without the prior written permission of the publisher.

Standard Book Number: 8096-1799-4
Library of Congress Catalog Card Number: 71-129428
Printed in the United States of America

ACKNOWLEDGMENTS

Many of the works from which selections herein are taken are protected by copyright, and may not be reproduced in any form without the consent of the authors, their publishers, or their agents. Every effort has been made to trace the ownership of all selections in this book and to obtain the necessary authorization for their use. If any errors or omissions have occurred in this regard, corrections will be made in all future editions of this book. Since the copyright page cannot legibly accommodate all the acknowledgments and copyright notices, this page and the pages following constitute an extension of the copyright page.

Grateful acknowledgment is made to:
Basic Books for selection by Gordon Allport quoted in *War*, ed. by Leon Bronson and George W. Goethals, 1968; China Books for selection by V. I. Lenin from *The State and Revolution*, 1965; Coward-McCann, Inc. for selection by Max Eastman from *Freedom in the Modern World*, 1928; Dell Publishing Co. for selection by John Lennon from *The Beatles Illustrated Lyrics*, 1969; by Eldridge Cleaver from *Soul on Ice*, 1968; Dodd, Mead and Company, Inc. for selection by Rupert Brooke from "The Soldier" in *The Collected Poems of Rupert Brooke*, 1915; Doubleday & Co., Inc. for selection by Peter L. Berger from *A Rumor of Angels*, 1969; by Marie Bashkirtseff from *Great Diaries*, 1957; E. P. Dutton & Co., Inc. for selection by Robert Kennedy from *Robert Kennedy: A Memoir* by Jack Newfield, 1969; Exposition

Press, Inc. for selection by Jack Schwartzman from *Rebels of Individualism,* 1949; Howard Fertig, Inc. for selection by Benito Mussolini from *The Ciano Diaries: 1939–1943,* 1943; Garrett Press, Inc. for selection by Francis Bacon from *The Complete Works of Sir Francis Bacon,* trans. by James Spedding, 1968; Grosset & Dunlap, Inc. for selection by Ernie Pyle from *Brave Men,* 1944; Harper & Row, Publishers for selection by Denis de Rougemont from *Man's Western Quest,* 1956; by Charles Frankel from *The Love of Anxiety and Other Essays,* 1951; by Aldous Huxley from *Ends and Means,* 1937; by Pierre Teilhard de Chardin from *The Divine Milieu,* 1960; by Thomas Wolfe from "Chickamauga" in *The Hills Beyond* by Thomas Wolfe, copyright © 1937 by Harper & Row and used by permission; Holt, Rinehart and Winston, Inc. from *The Poetry of Robert Frost* edited by Edward Connery Lathem. Copyright 1923 by Holt, Rinehart and Winston, Inc. Copyright 1951 by Robert Frost. Reprinted by permission of Holt, Rinehart and Winston, Inc.; by David Irving and Winston Churchill from David Irving's *The Destruction of Dresden,* 1964; Houghton Mifflin Company for selection by Daniel Bell from *Toward the Year 2000,* 1969; by Lord Moran from *Churchill: The Struggle for Survival,* 1966; by Adolf Hitler from *Mein Kampf,* trans. by R. Manheim, 1940; The Macmillan Company for selection by William Butler Yeats from "The Second Coming" in *Collected Poems,* copyright 1924 by The Macmillan Company, renewed 1952 by Bertha Georgie Yeats, and reprinted with the permission of The Macmillan Company; Modern Library, Inc. for selection by Miguel de Cervantes from *Don Quixote,* trans. Peter Anthony Motteux; The New American Library, Inc. for selection by Mariano Azuela from *The Underdogs;* New Directions Pub. Corp. for selection from Theodore Spencer's *The Paradox in the Circle.* Copyright 1941 by New Directions Publishing Corporation. Reprinted by permission of New Directions Publishing Corporation; Newman Press, Inc. for selection by Karl Rahner from *Do You Believe in God,* 1969; Nhan Dan and Quan Doi, Hanoi, for selection by General Vo Nguyen Giap from *The Big Victory, The Great Task,* 1967; W. W. Norton & Company, Inc. for selection by Rollo May from *Love and Will,* 1969; Frederick A. Praeger, Inc. for selection by Mao Tse-tung from *People's War,* trans. J. L. S. Girling, 1969; G. P. Putnam's Sons for selections by Jonas Ingram and Jean V. Dubois from Robert A. Heinlein's *Starship Troopers,* 1960; Quest Books, Inc. for selection by J. Krishnamurti from *Commentaries on Living, 2nd Series,* 1968; Random House, Inc. for selection by James Simon Kunen from *The Strawberry Statement,* 1969; by Jerome D. Frank from *Sanity and Survival,* 1968; by Robert Hillyer from *Thermopylae and Golgotha,* 1919; by Niccolo Machiavelli from *The Prince,* trans. by Luigi Ricci and R. P. Vincent, 1940; Henry Regnery Co. for selection by John Stuart Mill from *On Liberty of Thought and Discussion* (1859), 1959; Charles Scribner's Sons for selections by Ernest Hemingway from *From Whom the Bell Tolls,* 1940, and from *A Farewell to Arms,* 1929; by F. Scott Fitzgerald from *Note-Books;* The Seabury Press, Inc. for selection by Jacques Ellul from *Violence: Reflections From a Christian Perspective,* 1969; Simon & Schuster, Inc. for selection by Heywood Broun reprinted in J. & D. Berger's *Diary of America,* 1957; University of Chicago Press for selections by Donald Hagnall, William Tecumseh Sherman and Quincy Wright in Quincy Wright's *A Study of War,* 1964; The Viking Press, Inc. for selection by Arthur O'Shaughnessy's "Ode" from *The Portable Irish Reader,* 1946; by Elias Canetti from *Crowds and Power,* 1962.

Acknowledgment is gratefully made to the following periodicals and magazines:

Center Diary for selection by Gerald Sykes; *Collier's* for selection by Eugenio Pacelli; *Cross Currents* for selection by Abraham J. Heschel; *Esquire* for selections by Michael Kerr and Frank Conroy; *Look* for selections by J. Robert Moskin and John Poppy; *McCall's* for selection by Corita Kent; *The New York Times* for selections by Kenneth Kenniston, William L. Laurence, Donovan Leitch, David Low, Margaret Mead, Harrison E. Salisbury, and Charles Schulz; *Pace* for selections by Joan Baez, Art Buchwald, and Mason Williams; *Reader's Digest* for selections by Winston Churchill and Richard M. Nixon; *Sane* for selections by Tom Gardner, Jeffrey Martens, Gary Rader, and Bayard Rustin; *Time* for selections by Stanislav Andreski, Moshe Dayan, Linda Eldredge, Jerome D. Frank, Walter J. Hickel, Lyndon B. Johnson, Golda Meir, and Richard M. Nixon.

Photographs copyright © 1970 by Shelly Rusten. All rights reserved. Used by permission.

CONTENTS

Acknowledgments   5

Preface   11

PART I
Images of War   13

    1   Death
    2   Doomsday

PART II
The Pictures in Our Minds   47

    3   Ruffles and Flourishes
    4   Reactions
    5   Revolution
    6   Rational Analysis

PART III
The Possibility of Peace   147

    7   Beyond Nationalism
    8   A New Consciousness
    9   The Other Person
    10 The Future

Preface

The compilers and editors of this book, like all people on earth, want an end to war. As will be evident from the photographs, peace comes first in our thoughts and in our hopes. In *Peace, War and Youth* we did not intend to present our own personal views on the meaning of war and the way to peace. Rather we tried, first, to give an overview of the problem of war and the ways in which different people have seen and analyzed it; second, we tried to present views of the elements that enter into the shaping of a solution. In these pages, therefore, are found, side by side, the words of tyrants and patriots, allies and enemies, democrats and communists, soldiers and conscientious objectors, old men and children, religious men and atheists. What they all share in common is an awareness of what happens in war. Some of them have also considered ways to achieve peace.

PART I

IMAGES OF WAR

The earth turns. Day becomes night and today becomes yesterday. But every day there is war somewhere. Around the globe military advisers arrange tactical moves for their field forces. Radio networks hum with news of a new offensive launched against an enemy base. Intelligence sifts reports of enemy supply camps, missile sites, and jet raids. Ranger battalions knock out communications depots, supply caches, and military installations. Diplomats around peace conference tables accuse one another of unilateral aggression. Newspapers report lists of wounded and dead, week by week. An army nurse in Southeast Asia writes home of mutilated bodies of women and children. Suburban doves and hawks haggle with one another over an afternoon cocktail, while the air in the nearby city still holds traces of tear gas from last night's student riot.

Wherever one looks, he is surrounded by images of war: Pain, torture, tension, violence, crime, revolt, reaction, unrest, and conflict seem to be destroying human life. And the earth weeps as it turns . . .

1
DEATH

Beneath the rubble of a bomb-torn city and scattered upon a burned-out countryside lie human bodies, charred bodies, mutilated bodies, skeletons of bodies—empty of life, never to move or breathe again. Death is the strongest image of war. When the battle is over—or the riot or the border skirmish—the stretcher bearers come silently to carry away the slaughtered. In the distance, the ambulance grinds its siren, the church bells toll, the widow sobs her hopeless tears. All the earth groans in sorrow. The poet sadly sings of war: Who has decreed that agony and death should be the price of life?

Tears of rage and pain

Tears of rage and pain
rise to Demetrio's eyes
as Anastasio slowly slides
from his horse without a sound,
and lies outstretched, motionless.
Venancio falls close beside him,
his chest riddled with bullets.
Meco hurtles over the precipice,
bounding from rock to rock.

Suddenly Demetrio finds himself alone.
Bullets whiz past his ears like hail.
He dismounts and crawls over the rocks,
until he finds a parapet:
he lays down a stone to protect his head
and, lying flat on the ground,
begins to shoot.

The enemy scatter in all directions,
pursuing the few fugitives
hiding in the brush.
Demetrio aims;
he does not waste a single shot.
His famous marksmanship
fills him with joy.
Where he settles his glance,
he settles a bullet.
He loads his gun once more . . .
takes aim . . .

> Mariano Azuela
> *The Underdogs*

If it can do that to metal

Then it is night again, and the sky beyond the western perimeter is burning with slowly dropping magnesium flares. Heaps of equipment are on fire, terrifying in their jagged black massiveness, burning prehistoric shapes like the tail of a C-130 sticking straight up in the air, dead metal showing through the grey-black smoke. *God, if it can do that to metal, what will it do to me?* And then something very near me is smoldering, just above my head, the damp canvas coverings on the sandbags lining the top of a slit trench. It is a small trench, and a lot of us have gotten into it in a hurry. At the end farthest from me there is a young guy who has been hit in the throat, and he is making the sounds a baby will make who is trying to work up the breath for a good scream. We were on the ground when those rounds came . . .

A jeep pulled up to the dump and a Marine jumped out carrying a bunched-up fatigue jacket held out away from him. He looked very serious and scared. Some guy in his company, some guy he didn't even know, had been blown away right next to him, all over him. He held the fatigues up and I believed him. "I guess you couldn't wash them, could you?" I said. He really looked like he was going to cry as he threw them into the dump. "Man," he said, "you could take and scrub them fatigues for a million years, and *it would never happen.*"

Michael Kerr
"Khesanh"

We are the dead

When at last Judge Thayer in a tiny voice
passed sentence upon Sacco and Vanzetti,
a woman in the courtroom said with terror:
"It is death condemning life."

The men in the Charlestown prison
are shining spirits.
They are too bright,
we shield our eyes and kill them.
We are the dead,
and in us there is not feeling nor imagination
nor the terrible torment of lust for justice.

And in the city where we sleep
smug gardeners walk
to keep the grass above our little house sleek
and cut whatever blade thrusts up a head
above its fellows.

Heywood Broun

Fighting for ... ?

Then darkness enveloped the whole American armada. Not a pinpoint of light showed from those hundreds of ships as they surged on through the night toward their destiny, carrying across the ageless and indifferent sea tens of thousands of young men, fighting for ... for ... well, at least for each other.

Ernie Pyle

Somebody in that hole over there

It was the last week of the war and we were going along a road in southern Germany in a half-track and somebody said, "Hey—look over there, there's somebody in that hole over there in the field, shoot him!" So I swung the gun around—50 caliber—pressed the butterfly trigger, and nothing happened. Before I could load he came out with his hands up and I was sure glad I hadn't been able to shoot him.

Charles Schulz

You never get used to it

Sure, there were lots of bodies we never identified. You know what a direct hit by a shell does to a guy. Or a mine, or a solid hit with a grenade, even. Sometimes all we have is a leg or a hunk of arm.

The ones that stink the worst are the guys who got internal wounds and are dead about three weeks with the blood staying inside and rotting, and when you move the body the blood comes out of the nose and mouth. Then some of them bloat up in the sun, they bloat up so big that they bust the buttons and then they get blue and the skin peels. They don't all get blue, some of them get black.

But they all stink. There's only one stink and that's it. You never get used to it, either. As long as you live, you never get used to it. And after a while, the stink gets in your clothes and you can taste it in your mouth.

You know what I think? I think maybe if every civilian in the world could smell that stink, then maybe we wouldn't have any more wars.

Technical Sergeant Donald Haguall
48th Quartermaster Graves Registration
World War II

The American people

The American people
have a genius
for splendid
and unselfish action,
and into the hands
of America
God has placed
the destinies
of afflicted humanity.

Pope Pius XII (World War II)

Twenty-two million men under arms

In 35 centuries of recorded history,
only one year out of fifteen has not been drenched
by the blood of the battlefield.
Today, a world that presumably cherishes peace
as fervently as ever
nevertheless keeps 22 million men under arms—
many of them, as in Viet Nam and the Middle East,
actively engaged in combat.

Time Magazine

Hanoi on peace

Washington has never made a sincere offer of peace.
Whenever they carried out a so-called peace offensive,
they also intensified their aggression,
both in the North and in the South of our country.
It is criminal to deceive people this way.
Peace is not a game of politics.
Peace is the profound aspiration of all peoples.
I am sure that your American people want peace too.
But we will not sell our fundamental right
to independence for peace.
Independence and national unity are sacred to us.
I would have thought that the American people
would appreciate this.

Pham Van Dong
North Vietnamese Prime Minister (1967)

A lesson not yet learned

Americans, unique among the peoples on earth,
not only expect and prepare for war,
they expect and prepare to win any war they fight.
All other peoples have come to know defeat
and thus to be psychologically prepared for defeat,
invasion, occupation, humiliation,
knowing, too, that one day they will
overcome the occupant, free themselves
and forget the humiliation.
They are, therefore, psychologically prepared
for negotiation
and concession
and mutual compromise,
since they all have learned
how futile and temporary
the worst of defeats
or the most glorious of victories
is bound to be.
Americans alone have not learned this lesson yet.

David Schoenbrun

Statistics

World War I (1914–1918):
10,000,000 soldiers killed.
10,000,000 civilians killed.
20,000,000 wounded as a direct result
of hostilities.
20,000,000 dead as a result of
war-spread epidemics and famines
throughout the world.

World War II (1939–1945):
22,000,000 military and civilian dead.
34,000,000 wounded.

Korean War (1950–1953):
1,000,000 dead on both sides;
adding this to the civilian deaths
the total was 5,000,000.

Vietnam War (1954–19??):
Statistics still coming in.

Meanings

Acts of violence—
Whether on a large or a small scale,
the bitter paradox:
the meaningfulness of death—
and the meaninglessness of killing.

    Dag Hammarskjöld

Things have a terrible permanence
When people die.
    Aline Kilmer

2

DOOMSDAY

When will we have had our last April? Perhaps somewhere soon some nervous finger will push the ATTACK button, and a pulsing red light will indicate the start of the final nuclear holocaust. Or perhaps some worldwide radiation accident will happen, whose fallout will sterilize the planet. And the organic earth will decay and die of old age, never to see children—or Spring—again. And only the winds of space will record the failure of the great experiment: man.

But now a great fear is upon us . . .

> T. S. Eliot

For a moment

Let us reflect for a moment
on the horror . . .
All we say and do must be informed
by our awareness that this horror
is partly our responsibility . . .
It is our chemicals that scorch the children
and our bombs that level the villages.
We are all participants . . .
we must also feel as men the anguish
of what it is we are doing.

> Robert Kennedy

A continuing risk

Nothing is more certain and inexorable
than the law of chance.
Present policies involve
a continuing risk of nuclear war;
the longer the risk continues,
the greater the probability of war;
and if the probability continues long enough,
it approaches certainty.

       Jerome D. Frank

We need first of all to be thoroughly frightened.

       Harold Clayton Urey

The Atomic Age

The Atomic Age began
at exactly 5:30 Mountain War Time
on the morning of July 16, 1945,
on a stretch of semidesert land
about fifty airline miles from Alamogordo, New Mexico.

At that great moment in history,
ranking with the moment in the long ago
when man first put fire to work for him
and started on his march to civilization,
the vast energy locked within the hearts
of the atoms of matter was released
for the first time in a burst of flame
such as had never before been seen in this planet.

William L. Laurence

The doomsday clock

For nearly 25 years
the Bulletin of the Atomic Scientists
has carried on its cover a clock
showing man's closeness to total destruction.
Last year the hand was moved forward
to eight minutes to midnight,
eight minutes to N-hour.
The politicians and social scientists
of Russia, China and America
probably would agree on one thing:
Unless remarkably positive steps are taken
in the next five years,
the chances of the world celebrating
the dawn of New Year's in the year 2000
are far dimmer than at any moment
in recorded history;
possibly the chances of survival
are dimmer than in that cataclysmic moment
when the great age of glaciers dawned
and it must have seemed to many in that epoch
that the world would die in a girdle of ice
thousands of feet thick.

       Harrison E. Salisbury

A flood of barbarism and ruin

It is a truism that mankind's moral progress
has failed to keep pace with its scientific,
technical and cultural progress,
so that one of the possibilities,
which the future holds
is a flood of barbarism and ruin—
how far away or how near, none can tell.

                        Karl Rahner

I had learned

I had learned how to maim or kill a person
with my hands and feet
in a few seconds
and I was damned proud of it.
Suddenly one day I realized
what had happened to me,
and was disgusted.
The army having given me
a full appreciation of violence,
has turned me towards nonviolence
better than any other experience in my life.

                        Gary Rader

WE YOU HAVE
NOTHING TO
LOSE BUT YOUR
OUR
SONS + DAUGHTERS
CENTS
AND SOUL

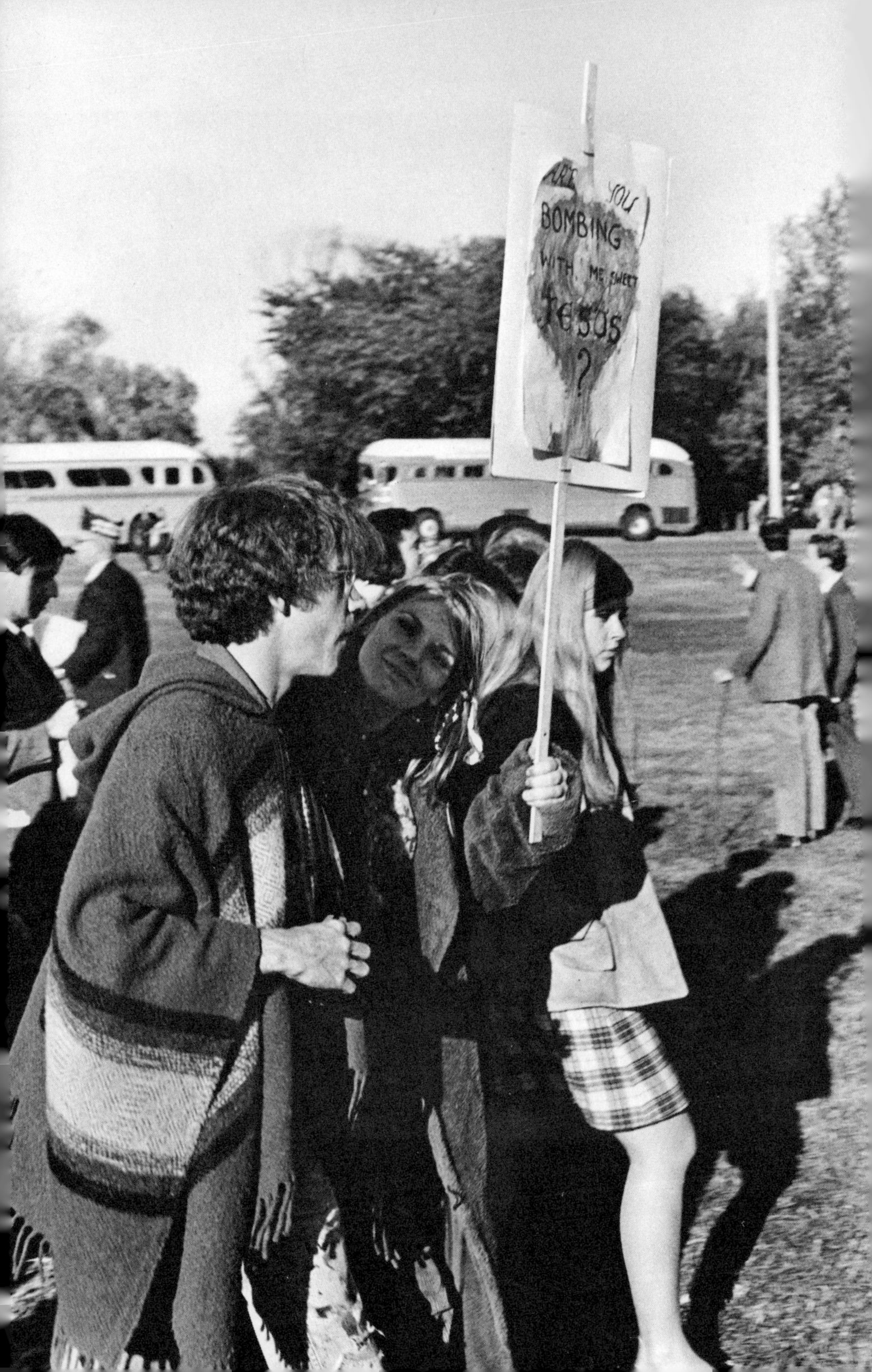
ARE YOU
BOMBING
WITH ME SWEET
JESUS
?

The appalling possibilities

To say that the world at present stinks
is to understate its fragrance.
To say that it must stink forever is a lie . . .

You do not have to be told
about the terrible threats of the present
which could lead to mass annihilation
and the savage end of civilization.
But you, better than most,
have been equipped to live
not only with but above
the appalling possibilities of our times.

                        John Mason Brown

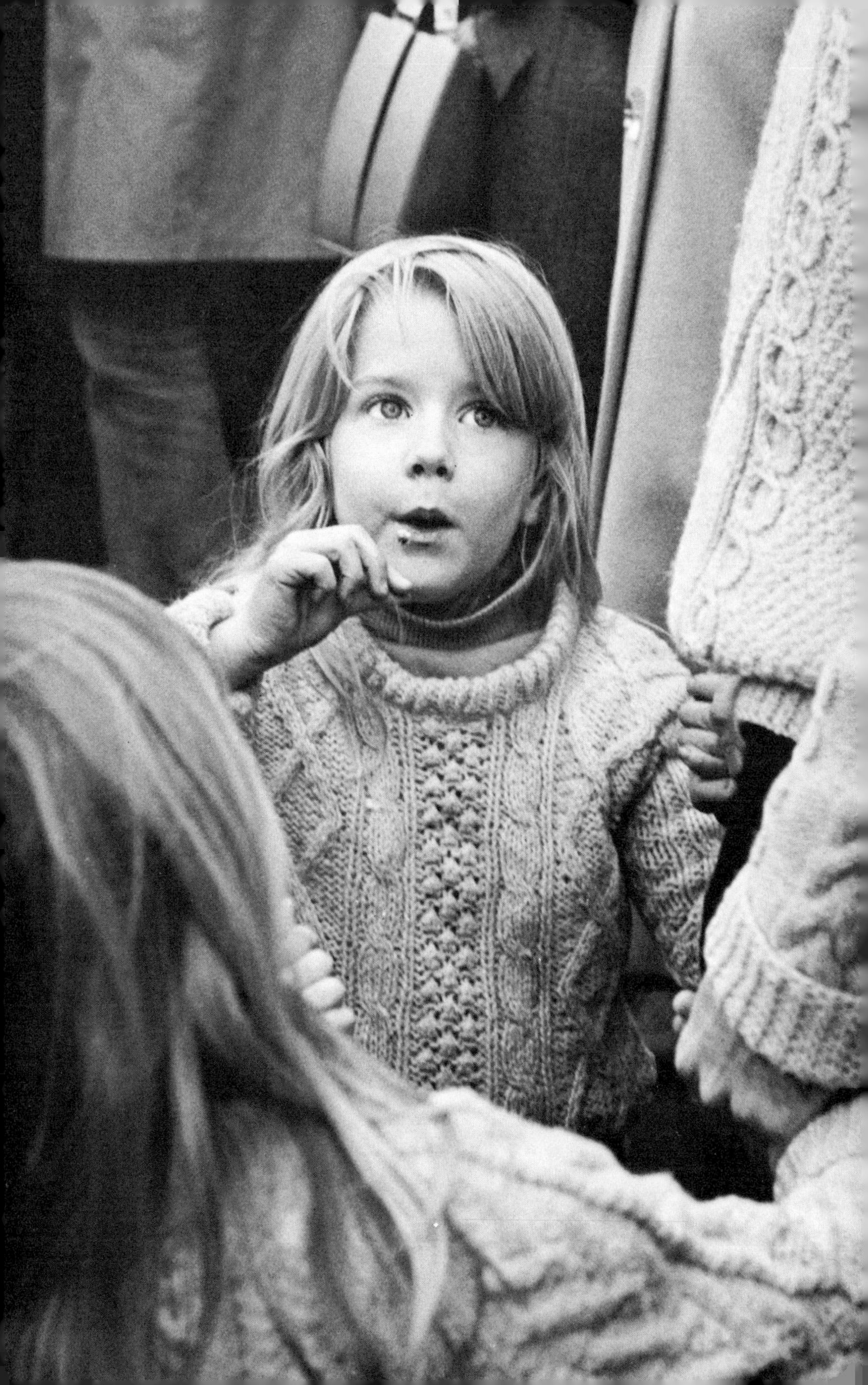

Power

Power is greater than it has ever been,
but also more precarious.
Today either every one will survive or no one.

> Elias Canetti

Genghis Khan

Genghis Khan had rare skill
in the organization and movement of men;
he planned a campaign
to its remotest details
and discussed it for weeks
with his marshals
before setting out;
a master strategist,
he avoided battle when unnecessary,
and moved directly
to the annihilation of the center of resistance,
and the death of the opposing leader.
Terror and secrecy
surrounded his movements
and behind him
he left a hideous toll of dead.

> Harold Lamb

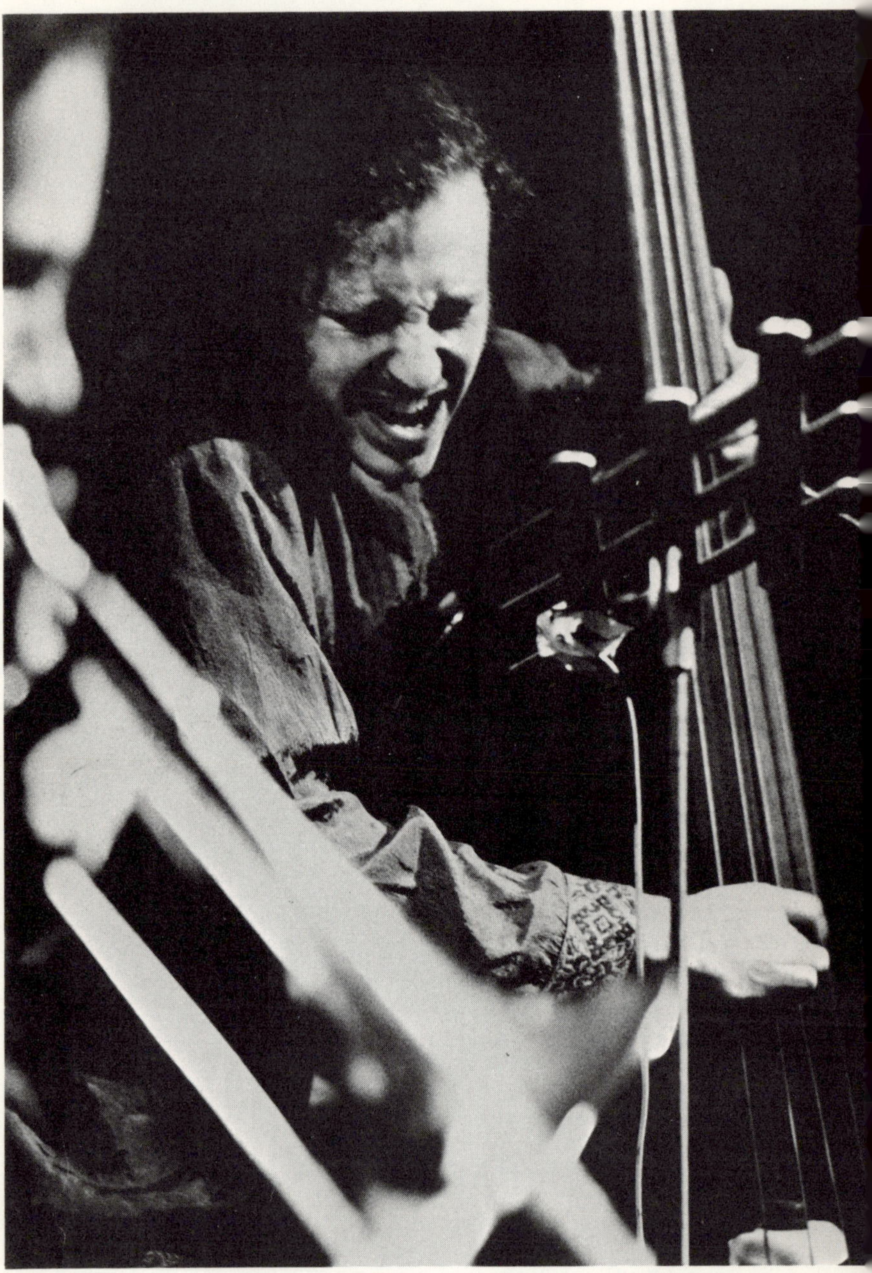

For whom the bell tolls

Any man's death diminishes me,
because I am involved in Mankind;
And therefore never send to know
   for whom the bell tolls;
It tolls for thee.

                    John Donne

The unique part

Once the moral person has been killed,
the one thing that still prevents men
from being made into living corpses
is the differentiation of the individual,
his unique identity . . . there is no doubt
that this part of the human person,
precisely because it depends so essentially
on nature and on forces
that cannot be controlled by the will,
is the hardest to destroy
(and when destroyed is the most easily repaired).

                    Hannah Arendt

PART II

THE PICTURES IN OUR MINDS

People are not all alike. There is no "ordinary man in the street," no "average housewife," no "typical teen-ager." My world is not the same as yours. People may live in the same country, in the same state, in the same town; they may go to the same school, work in the same office or shop, watch the same programs on television. But they still think and respond differently. "Two men looked out through prison bars; one saw mud, the other stars." Each person is really different from each other person. Each has his own way of seeing and interpreting a burning draft card or the decisions of a national leader.

The search for meaning, for a new order, for a way out of war, takes on various shapes—some hopeful, some threatening. The awareness of emergency gives rise to urgency. Mistaken images must be corrected, fixed ideas must be made pliable, dead concepts must be carried off and buried. Many minds visualize the ways things could be. Often these visualizations are conflicting and contradictory. The road to peace is not an easy one.

3
RUFFLES AND FLOURISHES

The drums roll, the trumpets blow their fanfare, the guns salute the presence of the makers of war. Surrounded by ceremonial horses, protected by a military color guard with polished rifles, amid waving flags and the paraphernalia of war, they stand erect, decorated with medals and stars, the symbols of power and command. Do their words show a concern for peace? When they are far from the battleground and alone do they weep in sorrow and compassion? Do they hear man's cry for no more war?

On Tamerlane's tomb in Samarkand

This is the resting place
of the illustrious and merciful
    monarch,
the most great Sultan,
the most mighty Warrior,
Lord Timur, conqueror of the
    Earth.

Those who build

Unless the Lord
builds the house,
those who build it
labor in vain . . .

>   Psalm 127

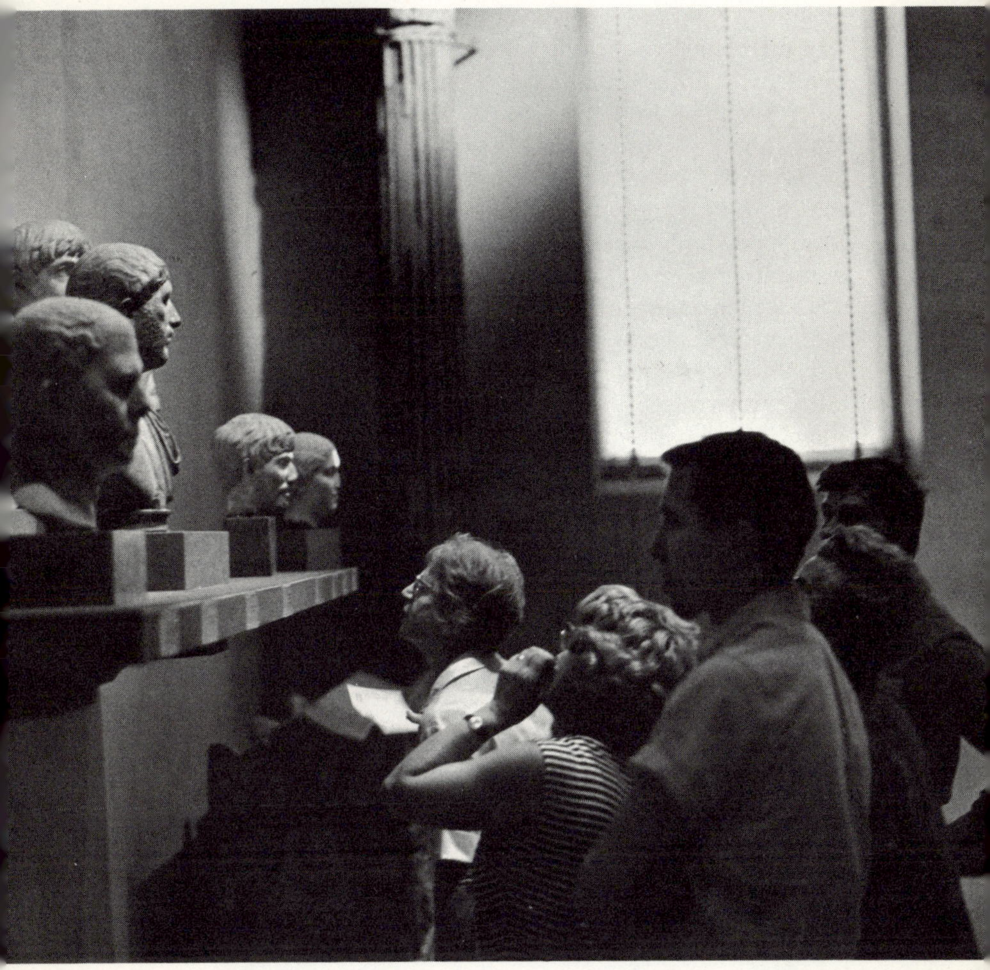

The fox and the lion

You must know, then, that there are two methods of fighting, the one by law, the other by force: the first method is that of men, the second of beasts; but as the first method is often insufficient, one must have recourse to the second ...

A prince being thus obliged to know well how to act as a beast must imitate the fox and the lion, for the lion cannot protect himself from traps, and the fox cannot defend himself from wolves. One must therefore be a fox to recognize traps, and a lion to frighten wolves. Those that wish to be only lions do not understand this. Therefore, a prudent ruler ought not to keep faith when by so doing it would be against his interest, and when the reasons which made him bind himself no longer exist. If men were all good, this precept would not be a good one; but as they are bad, and would not observe their faith with you, so you are not bound to keep faith with them. Nor have legitimate grounds ever failed a prince who wished to show colorable excuse for the nonfulfillment of his promise. Of this one could furnish an infinite number of modern examples, and show how many times the peace has been broken, and how many promises rendered worthless, by the faithlessness of princes, and those that have been best able to imitate the fox have succeeded best. But it is necessary to be able to disguise this character well, and to be a great feigner and dissembler; and men are so simple and so ready to obey present necessities, that one who deceives will always find those who allow themselves to be deceived.

Niccolo Machiavelli

Victory over reason

The one means that wins
the easiest victory over reason:
terror and force.

Adolf Hitler

We've got no place in this outfit
for good losers.
We want tough hombres
who will go in there and win!

        Admiral Jonas Ingram

At all costs

Victory at all costs, victory in spite of all terror, victory however long and hard the road may be; for without victory there is no survival ...

We shall defend every village, every town and every city. The vast mass of London itself, fought street by street, could easily devour an entire hostile army: And we would rather see London laid in ruins and ashes than that it should be tamely and abjectly enslaved.

Winston Churchill

Like a mighty storm

In a very short time, in China's central, southern and northern provinces, several hundred million peasants will rise like a mighty storm ... so swift and violent that no power, however great, will be able to hold it back. ... They will sweep all the imperialists, warlords, corrupt officials, local tyrants and evil gentry into their graves. Every revolutionary party and every revolutionary comrade will be put to the test. ... There are three alternatives. To march at their head and lead them? To trail behind them, gesticulating and criticizing? Or to stand in their way and oppose them? Every Chinese is free to choose, but events will force you to make the choice quickly.

Mao Tse-tung (1927)

The Assassins

So when the Old Man wanted any Prince slain,
he would say to such a youth:
"Go and slay So-and-So;
and when you return
my Angels shall bear you into Paradise.
And if you should die,
I will nonetheless send my Angels
to carry you back into Paradise."
So he caused them to believe;
and thus there was no order of his
that they would not confront
any peril to execute,
because of their great desire
to get back into that Paradise of his.
And in this manner
the Old One got his people to murder
anyone he desired to get rid of.
Thus, too, the great dread
that he inspired in all Princes
made them become his tributaries
in order that he might abide
at peace and amity with them.

        Marco Polo

There is nothing I would not give
if I could promise you peace,
but I cannot promise it.

> Golda Meir

We have finished warning the Americans
and the Zionists ...
We are about to start fighting them
in earnest.

> Arab Commando

Israel must take action
across the border.

> Moshe Dayan

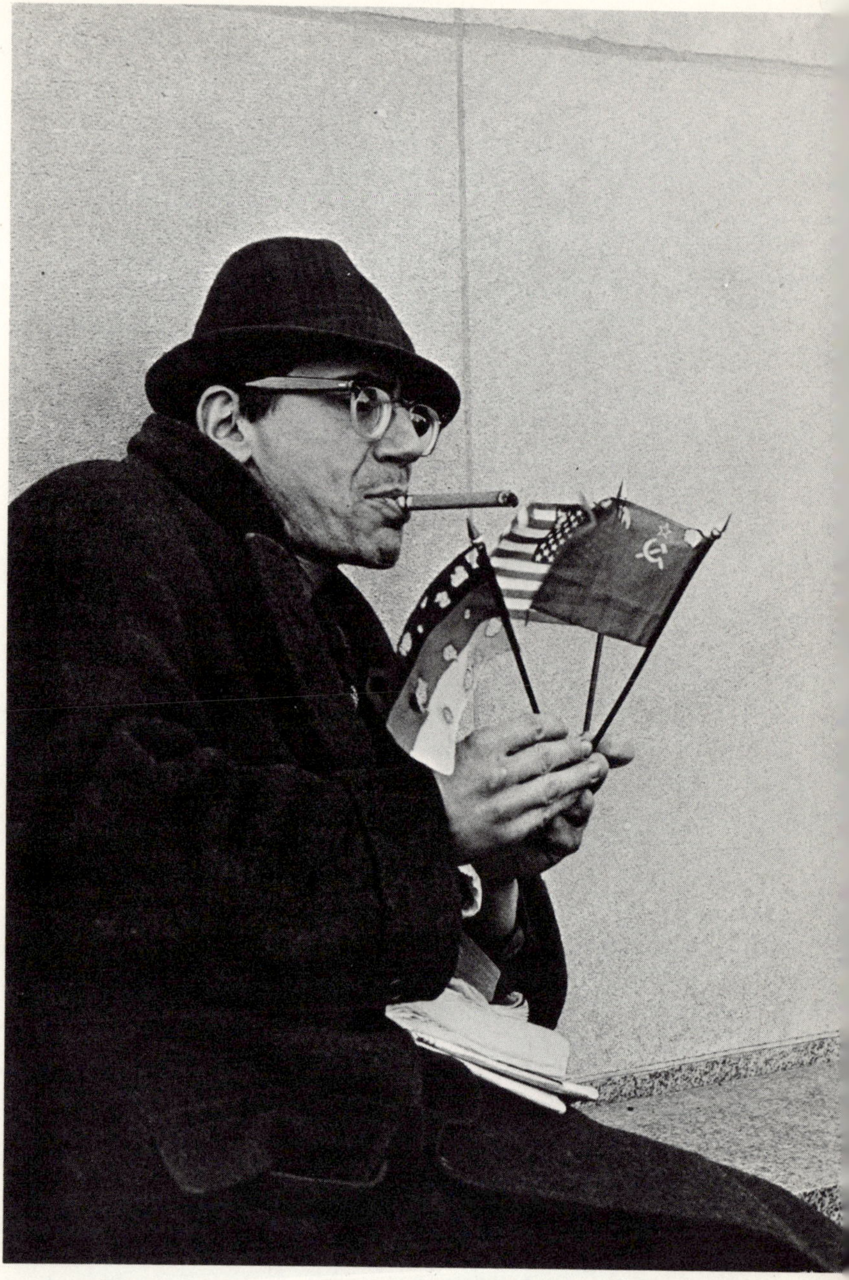

To the enemy

In case of a forced retreat of Red Army units, all rolling stock must be evacuated; to the enemy must not be left a single engine, a single railway car, not a single pound of grain or a gallon of fuel. . . . In occupied regions conditions must be made unbearable for the enemy and all his accomplices. They must be hounded and annihilated at every step and all their measures frustrated.

Joseph Stalin
The "Scorched Earth" Address

A valuable mark of sympathy

Our people highly appreciate the struggle of the American people against the aggressive Vietnamese war of the Johnson Administration, considering it a valuable mark of sympathy and support for our people's just resistance. Moreover, our people are thoroughly aware that the decisive factor in the success of the anti-U.S. national-salvation resistance is our people's objective performance on the Vietnam battlefield, where there is a firm struggle between the aggressors and the victims of aggression, and where the war situation is increasingly favorable to the heroic South Vietnamese people. Our people hold that after the forthcoming presidential election in the United States, despite a possible change of presidents, the nature of the U.S. imperialists' aggressive policy will remain the same. The U.S. presidential elections will make the American people more aware of the errors and setbacks of the Johnson Administration in the aggressive war in Vietnam, and so the struggle of the American people against the aggressive war will become stronger.

> General Vo Nguyen Giap
> on Radio Hanoi (1967)

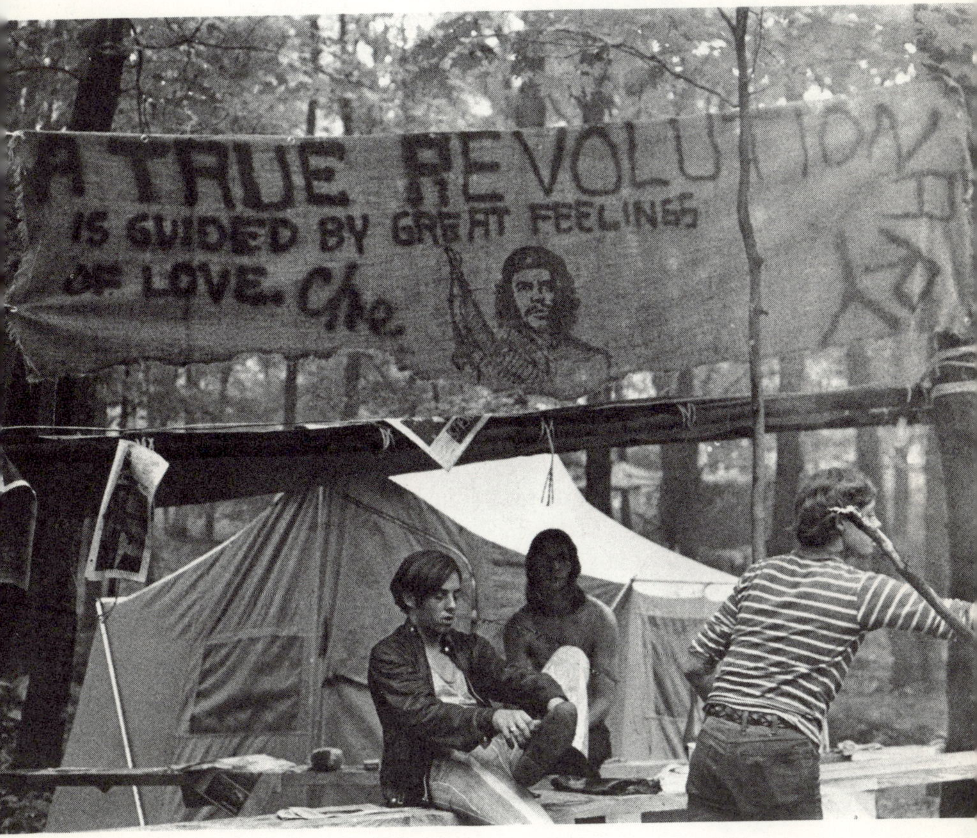
A TRUE REVOLUTION
IS GUIDED BY GREAT FEELINGS
OF LOVE. Che.

But he likes to kill

Capt. Binh is a Vietnamese officer attached to your company. He's a good soldier, but he likes to kill. He's been in too long. A couple of sergeants are guarding VC prisoners, five of them. They've been stripped. Then two old women, suspected VCs, are sent back. "Shall we strip 'em, lieutenant?" one of the sergeants asks. He'd like to. "No. Search 'em, but don't strip 'em." Capt. Binh comes in and starts interrogating the prisoners one by one. He beats them up some. When he gets to the first old woman she reaches under her skirt and pulls out a grenade. There isn't time to do anything but watch Binh and the old woman dissolve in a hail of shrapnel. The sentries and Binh's men empty their automatic rifles into the remaining prisoners and the noise is deafening. The old woman was able to kill Binh because you hadn't stripped her. If you had stripped her, Binh would be alive now—and so would the prisoners. You are sick. You are embarrassed and you feel ashamed.

Charles Coe
Young Man in Vietnam

Statements

We could no longer
stand by
while attacks mounted
and while the bases
of the attackers
were immune from reply.

If we are driven
from the field
in Viet Nam,
then no nation
can ever again
have the same confidence
in American promise
or in American protection.

Our conclusions are plain.
We will not surrender.
We do not wish
to enlarge the conflict.
We desire
peaceful settlement
and talks.

The United States
still seeks no wider war.

        Lyndon B. Johnson

We will not allow
American men
by the thousands
to be killed by an enemy
from privileged
sanctuaries.

If we did, credibility
of the United States
would be destroyed
in every area of the world
where only the power
of the United States
deters aggression.

We will be conciliatory
at the conference table,
but we will not
be humiliated.
We will not be defeated.

We shall avoid
a wider war.

        Richard M. Nixon

A good many things
go around in the dark
besides Santa Claus.

    Herbert Hoover

Shoot first
and inquire afterwards,
and if you
make mistakes,
I will protect you.

    Hermann Goering

He had never been to Dresden

The Master Bomber for the second Dresden attack
was a very experienced pilot,
with more than three tours
of operations behind him;
once, in November 1944, he had been asked
to act as Master Bomber
during the disastrous attack
on Freiburg im Breisgau,
but he had declined,
as he had studied at the University there
and had many friends in the area
around the Freiburg Cathedral
which was to be the aiming point for the attack;
he had, however, never been to Dresden,
and although he deeply regretted
the necessity for the destruction
of such a fine and beautiful city,
he could find no personal reason
for objecting.

       David Irving

The NLF on the United States

The U.S. imperialists are daily causing untold sufferings and mourning to our compatriots throughout the country! They have resorted to all kinds of modern war means and weapons, including strategic aircraft, napalm bombs, toxic chemicals, and poison gas to massacre our fellow countrymen. They have launched repeated operations, again and again sweeping many areas, carrying out the kill all, burn all, destroy all policy to raze villages and hamlets to the ground. They have herded the population, grabbed land, and set up a no-man's land and fascist-type concentration camps dubbed strategic hamlets, prosperity zones, resettlement areas, and so on. In the north, they have wantonly bombed and strafed streets, villages, industrial centers, and heavily populated areas. They have even struck at dikes, dams, schools, hospitals, churches and pagodas.

Obviously the U.S. imperialists are the most ruthless aggressors in history, the saboteurs of the 1954 Geneva agreements, the saboteurs of the peace and security of the peoples in Indochina, Southeast Asia, and the world —the enemy number one of our people and of mankind ...

The U.S. aggressors and their lackeys think they can intimidate our people by the use of force and deceive them by means of tricks. But they are grossly mistaken. Our people will definitely never submit to force, never let themselves be deceived! Bringing into play our nation's tradition of undauntedness, our 31 million compatriots from the south to the north have resolutely stood up and united as one man to fight against the U.S. aggressors and save the country.

On the front line of the fatherland, our southern fellow countrymen have over the past 13 years shown marvelous heroism. Irrespective of age, sex, political tendencies, religious beliefs, and no matter whether they live in the plains or in mountain areas, our people of all strata and all nationalities have resolutely fought shoulder to shoulder to liberate the south, defend the north, and proceed toward the reunification of the fatherland ...

Political Program
National Liberation Front

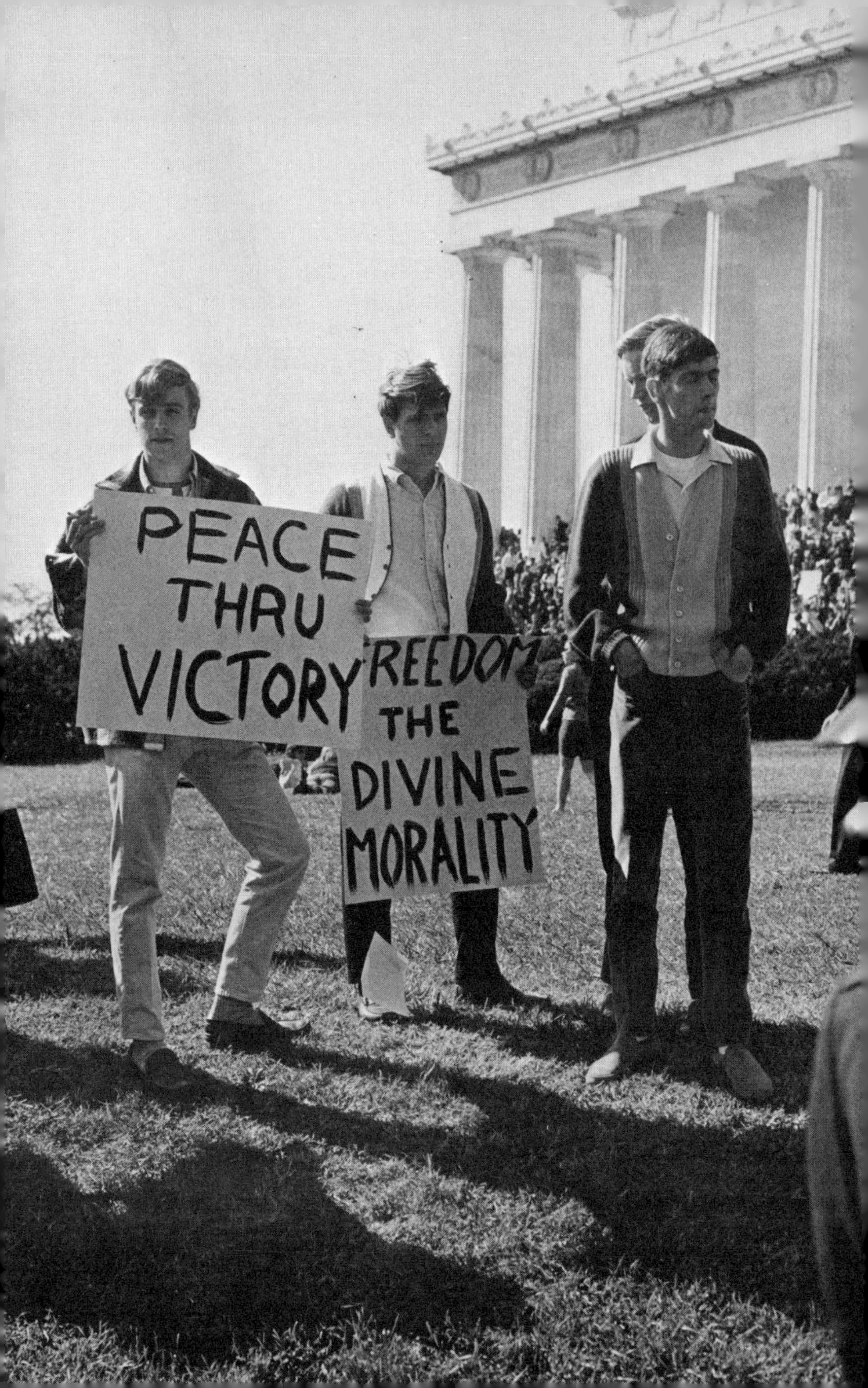
PEACE
THRU
VICTORY
FREEDOM
THE
DIVINE
MORALITY

Consider the consequences

I respect the right of each American
to express his own opinion.
I recognize that many feel
a moral obligation to express their opinions
in the most conspicuous way possible.
I respect that.

However, as President,
my responsibility is different.
I must consider the consequences
of each proposed course of action—
short-term and long-term
domestic and worldwide, direct and indirect.
Others can say of Vietnam, "Get out now";
when asked how, they can give
the simple, flip answer: "By sea."
They can ignore the consequences.
But as I consider those consequences,
in both human and international terms,
I can only conclude that history
would rightly condemn a President
who took such a course.

We are on the road to peace.
That road is not easy.
It is not simple.
But I am convinced that it is the right one.

                        Richard M. Nixon

Men lied to them,
and so they went to die.

          Robert Hillyer

If an idea is right in itself,
and if thus armed
it embarks on the struggle
in this world,
it is invincible
and every persecution
will lead to its inner strengthening.

          Adolf Hitler

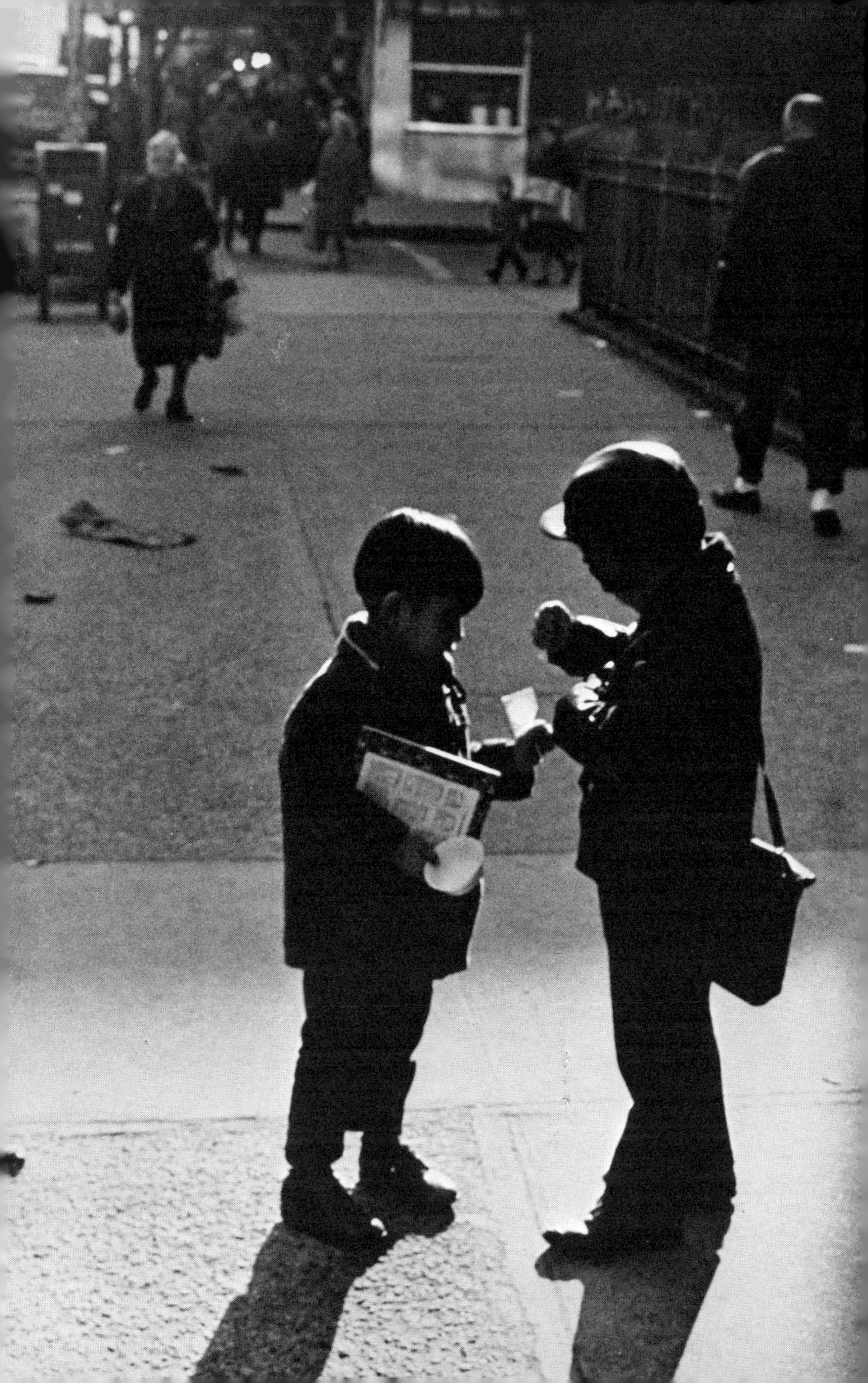

War
is the supreme test
of man, in which he rises
to heights
never approached
in any other activity.

General George S. Patton

War alone brings up
to its highest tension
all human energy
and puts the stamp
of nobility
upon the peoples
who have the courage
to face it.

Benito Mussolini

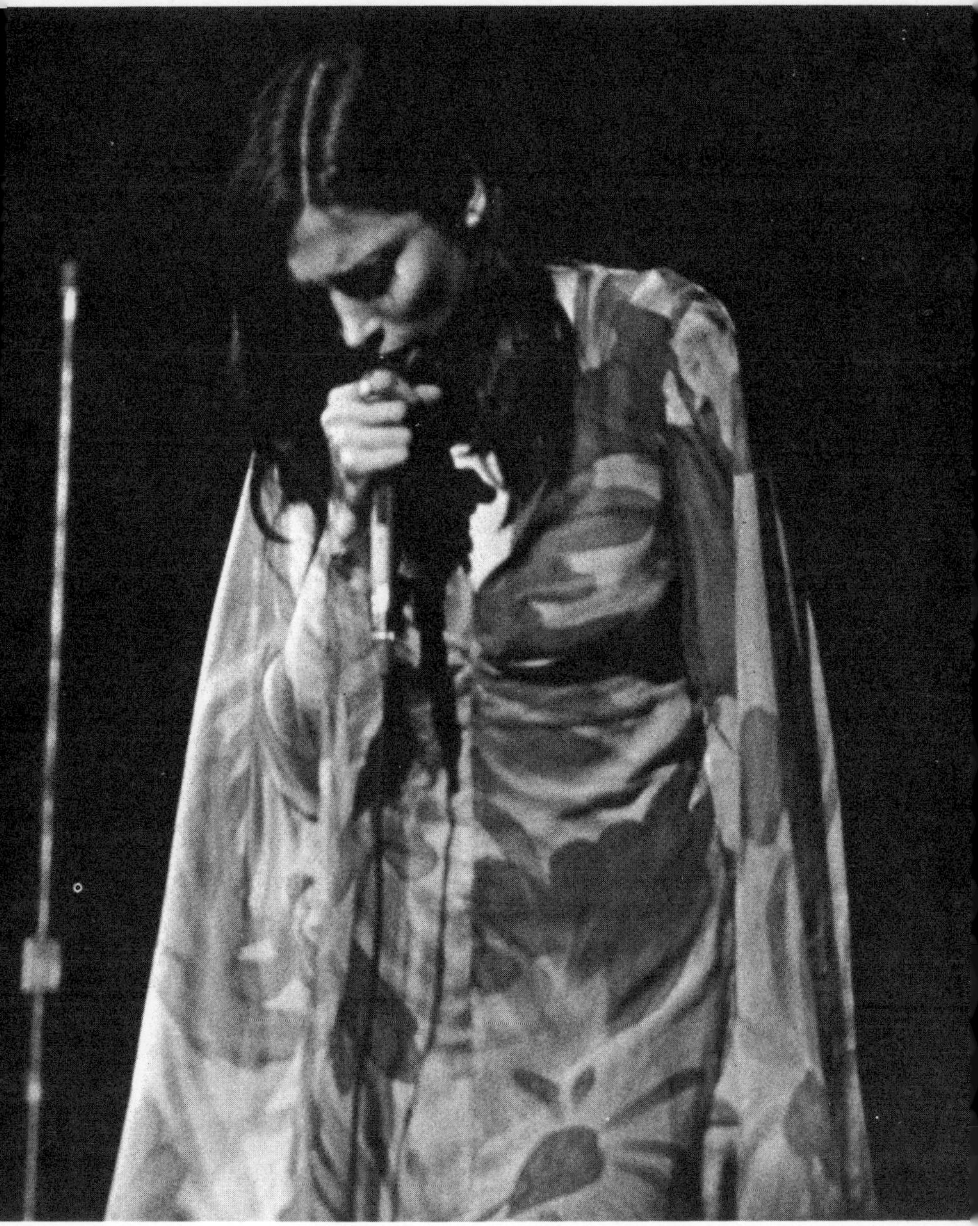

The highest moment

To die at the height of a man's career,
the highest moment of his effort
here in this world,
universally honored and admired,
to die while great issues
are still commanding
the whole of his interest,
to be taken from us
at a moment when he could already see
ultimate success in view—
is not the most unenviable of fates.

> Winston Churchill

It is sweet and honorable
to die for one's country.

> Horace

In the final choice
a soldier's pack
is not so heavy a burden
as a prisoner's chains.

Dwight David Eisenhower

Show me a hero
and I will write you a tragedy.

        F. Scott Fitzgerald

It is entirely compatible with his genius
that it should have occurred
to Albert Einstein
to address a formal inquiry
to Sigmund Freud
regarding the psychological principles
involved in war.

"How is it possible," he asked,
"for the ruling minority
to force the masses
to observe a purpose
which rewards them only
with suffering and loss?
Why do the masses permit themselves
to be inflamed to the point of madness
and self-sacrifice
by these means . . . ?"

        Karl A. Menninger

PLEASE REMAIN. YOU FURNISH THE PICTURES AND I'LL FURNISH THE WAR.

> William Randolph Hearst
> Telegram to Frederic Remington,
> when Remington wished to return
> home from Cuba.
> March, 1898

Man, proud man

> ... but man, proud man,
> Dress'd in a little brief authority,
> Most ignorant of what he's most assur'd—
> His glassy essence—like an angry ape,
> Plays such fantastic tricks before high heaven
> As make the angels weep ...
>
> William Shakespeare
> *Measure for Measure*

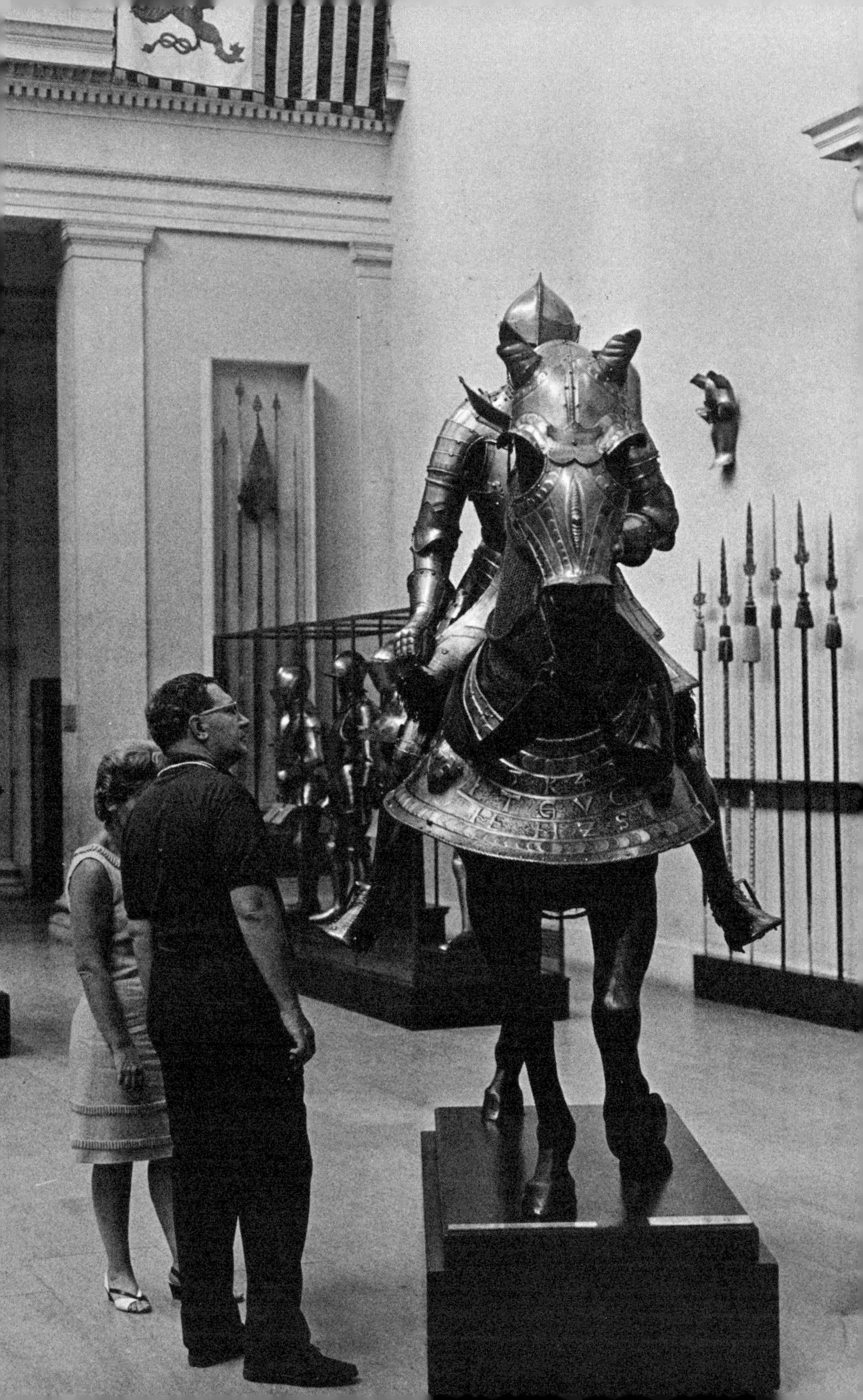

4

REACTIONS

Campus sit-ins, labor walkouts, antiwar protests, prowar demonstrations. Giant father figures revealing deep-seated hostilities beneath their hats or in their cool rhetoric. Schoolchildren reacting violently as their older brothers march off to the draft. Conscientious objectors facing the charge of anti-patriotism. Old soldiers telling stories of war years: excitement, bravery, comradeship, how men died nobly for their families and country. A new generation reacts differently. They do battle for peace with posters, buttons, bumper stickers, slogans, picket lines, and petitions. At every turn, on street corners, in newspapers and magazines, on radio and television, politicians, psychologists, poets, schoolteachers, novelists, military men—all express strong feelings about war and peace.

Others in his place

There are two things
the American government can take away
from the American citizen.
It can take his money, in taxes.
And it can take his body,
for services in the armed forces—
which can mean taking his life.
The taxing power is exercised
in such a way that a rich man
who uses money to make money,
can avoid paying anything
like his fair share of taxes . . .
A young man who exploits the system
to duck the draft or avoid combat
is only being sensible.
But he can never quite shake off
the knowledge that others
are being shouted at
or shot at in his place.
In such circumstances, it is not really hard
to see why many young men feel
a psychic need to believe
that America's role in Vietnam
is wholly "obscene,"
and to believe also
that the whole American system
is rotten and corrupt.

Stewart Alsop

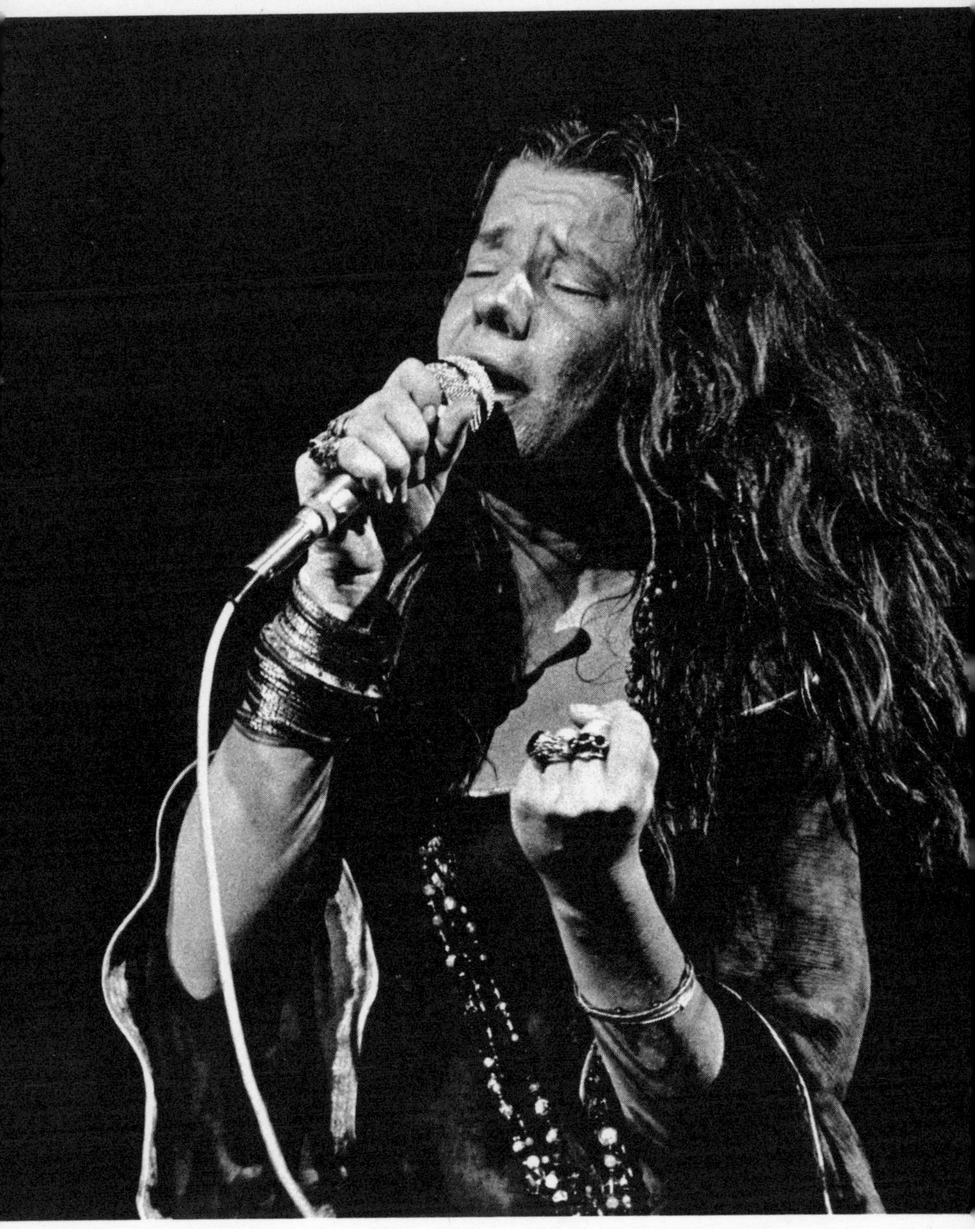

The four horsemen of the Apocalypse

Now I saw when the Lamb
opened one of the seven seals,
and I heard one
of the four living creatures say,
as with a voice of thunder, "Come!"
And I saw, and behold,
a white horse, and its rider had a bow;
and a crown was given to him,
and he went out conquering and to conquer.

When he opened the second seal,
I heard the second living creature say, "Come!"
And out came another horse,
bright red; its rider was permitted
to take peace from the earth,
so that men should slay one another;
and he was given a great sword.

When he opened the third seal,
I heard the third living creature say, "Come!"
And I saw, and behold,
a black horse, and its rider
had a balance in his hand;
and I heard what seemed to be
a voice in the midst of the four living creatures
saying, "A quart of wheat for a denarius,
and three quarts of barley for a denarius;
but do not harm oil and wine!"

When he opened the fourth seal,
I heard the voice
of the fourth living creature say, "Come!"
And I saw, and behold, a pale horse,

and its rider's name was Death,
and Hades followed him;
and they were given power
over a fourth of the earth,
to kill with sword
and with famine
and with pestilence
and by wild beasts of the earth.

When he opened the fifth seal,
I saw under the altar the souls
of those who had been slain for the word of God
and for the witness they had borne ...

Revelation 6:1–9

Love and war

Love and War are the same thing,
and stratagems and policy are as allowable
in the one as in the other.

Miguel de Cervantes

An immortal truth

The noblest fate
that a man can endure
is to place
his own mortal body
between his loved home
and the war's desolation.
The words are not mine,
of course, as you
will recognize.
Basic truths cannot change
and once a man of insight
expresses one of them
it is never necessary,
no matter how much
the world changes,
to reformulate them.
This is an immutable truth,
true everywhere,
throughout all time,
for all men
and all nations.

> Robert A. Heinlein
> *Starship Troopers*

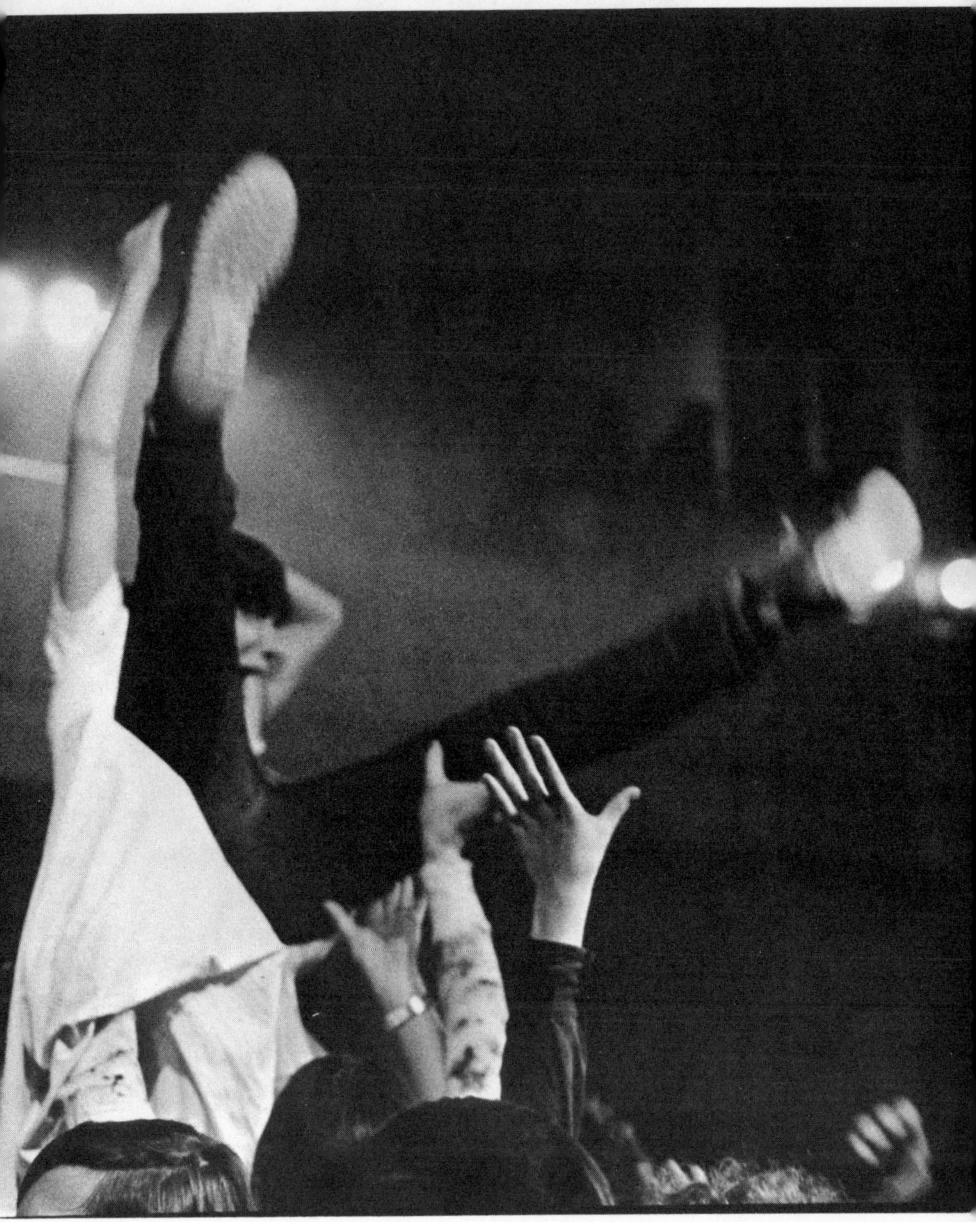

Come on,
you sons
of bitches!
Do you want
to live
forever?

Army Sergeant
  World War I

I see that the old flagpole still stands.
Have your troops hoist the colors to its peak,
and let no enemy ever haul them down.

                                      Douglas MacArthur

The Armageddon day

He wouldn't have missed that war for anything. Back didn't go to war because he wanted to kill Yankees. He didn't want to kill nobody. He was as tenderhearted as a baby and as brave as a lion. Some fellers told hit on him later how they'd come on him at Gettysburg, shootin' over a stone wall, and his rifle bar'l had got so hot he had to put hit down and rub his hands on the seat of his pants because they got so blistered. He was singin' hymns, they said, with tears a-streamin' down his face—that's the way they told hit, anyway—and every time he fired he'd sing another verse. And I reckon he killed plenty because when Back had a rifle in his hands he didn't miss.

But he was a good man. He didn't want to hurt a fly. And I reckon the reason that he went to war was because he thought he'd be at Armageddon. That's the way he had hit figgered out, you know. When the war came, Back said: "Well, this is hit, and I'm a-goin' to be thar. The hour has come," he said, "when the Lord is goin' to set up His kingdom here on earth and separate the sheep upon the right hand and the goats upon the left—jest like hit was predicted long ago—and I'm a-goin' to be thar when hit happens."

Well, we didn't ask him which side *he* was goin' to be on, but we all knowed which side without havin' to ask. Back was goin' to be on the *sheep* side—that's the way he had hit figgered out right up to the day of his death ten years ago. He kept prophesyin' and predictin' right up to the end. No matter what happened, no matter what mistakes he made, he kept right on predictin'. First he said the war was goin' to be the Armageddon day. And when that didn't happen he said hit was goin' to come along in the eighties. And when hit didn't happen then he moved hit up to the nineties. And when the war broke out in 1914 and the whole world had to go, why Bacchus knowed that *that* was hit.

And no matter how hit all turned out, Back never would give in or own up he was wrong. He'd say he'd made a mistake in his figgers somers, but that he'd found out what hit was and that next time he'd be right. And that's the way he was up to the time he died.

Thomas Wolfe
"Chickamauga"

Life

Wars with their noise affright us: when they cease,
    We are worse in peace:
What then remains, but that we still should cry
    Not to be born, or, being born, to die?

                          Francis Bacon

The Soldier

If I should die, think only this of me:
That there's some corner of a foreign field
That is for ever England. There shall be
In that rich earth a richer dust concealed;
A dust whom England bore, shaped, made aware.
Gave, once, her flowers to love, her ways to roam,
A body of England's, breathing English air,
Washed by the rivers, blest by suns of home.
And think, this heart, all evil shed away,
A pulse in the eternal mind, no less
Gives somewhere back the thoughts by England given;
Her sights and sounds; dreams happy as her day;
And laughter, learnt of friends; and gentleness,
In hearts at peace, under an English heaven.

                          Rupert Brooke

Right or wrong

Our country, right or wrong.
When right, to be kept right;
When wrong, to be put right.

Carl Schurz

Man is unique

War is a purely human phenomenon.
The lower animals fight duels
in the heat of sexual excitement
and kill for food
and occasionally for sport. . . .
Man is unique in organizing
the mass murder of his own species.

Aldous Huxley

The memory of wartime

I remember asking, as a very young child, what was in the newspapers when there wasn't a war going on. That was the Second World War, the war to eradicate evil from the face of the earth, the war in which all Americans believed. Victory gardens, V-Mail, Gold Star Mothers, ration books and air-raid drills were the order of the day. People talked lustfully of three-inch-thick steaks, automobile tires and real butter. My father carried in his vest pocket his own personal sugar dispenser for coffee and my mother could be reduced to tears by a run in her stockings. The rationing of food, the enemy without, common hardship, common purpose and the almost godlike presence of Franklin Delano Roosevelt served to unify the country as it had perhaps never been unified before. If the First World War, however bloody, had been a bit of a lark, the Second was quite clearly a war of survival. Americans did not expect to lose, yet they knew they'd have to fight like hell to win. The discovery of the death camps of Central Europe resolved all questions as to what the war had been about. The forces of light against the forces of darkness, that was what we believed, and no American thirty-two years old can be untouched by that memory.

Frank Conroy
"My Generation"

An affirmation

Just before the Soviet troops
occupied Vienna in 1945,
the Vienna Philharmonic
gave one of its scheduled concerts.
There was fighting
in the immediate proximity of the city,
and the concertgoers could hear
the rumbling of the guns in the distance.
The entry of the Soviet army
interrupted the concert schedule—
if I'm not mistaken, for about a week.
Then the concerts resumed, as scheduled.
In the universe of this particular play,
the world shattering events
of the Soviet invasion,
the overthrow of one empire
and the cataclysmic appearance of another,
meant a small interruption in the program.
Was this simply a case of callousness,
of indifference to suffering?
Perhaps in the case of some individuals,
but, basically, I would say not.
It was rather an affirmation
of the ultimate triumph of all human gestures
of creative beauty
over the gestures of destruction,
and even over the ugliness
of war and death.

                                               Peter L. Berger

Friend and foe

Young people today are unable to see
the killing of an enemy as different
from the murder of one's own children,
and they cannot reconcile the efforts
to save our own children by every means,
with our willingness to pour napalm
on other people's children.
Older distinctions between "friend and foe,"
simply do not make the kind of sense
that they once made.

Margaret Mead

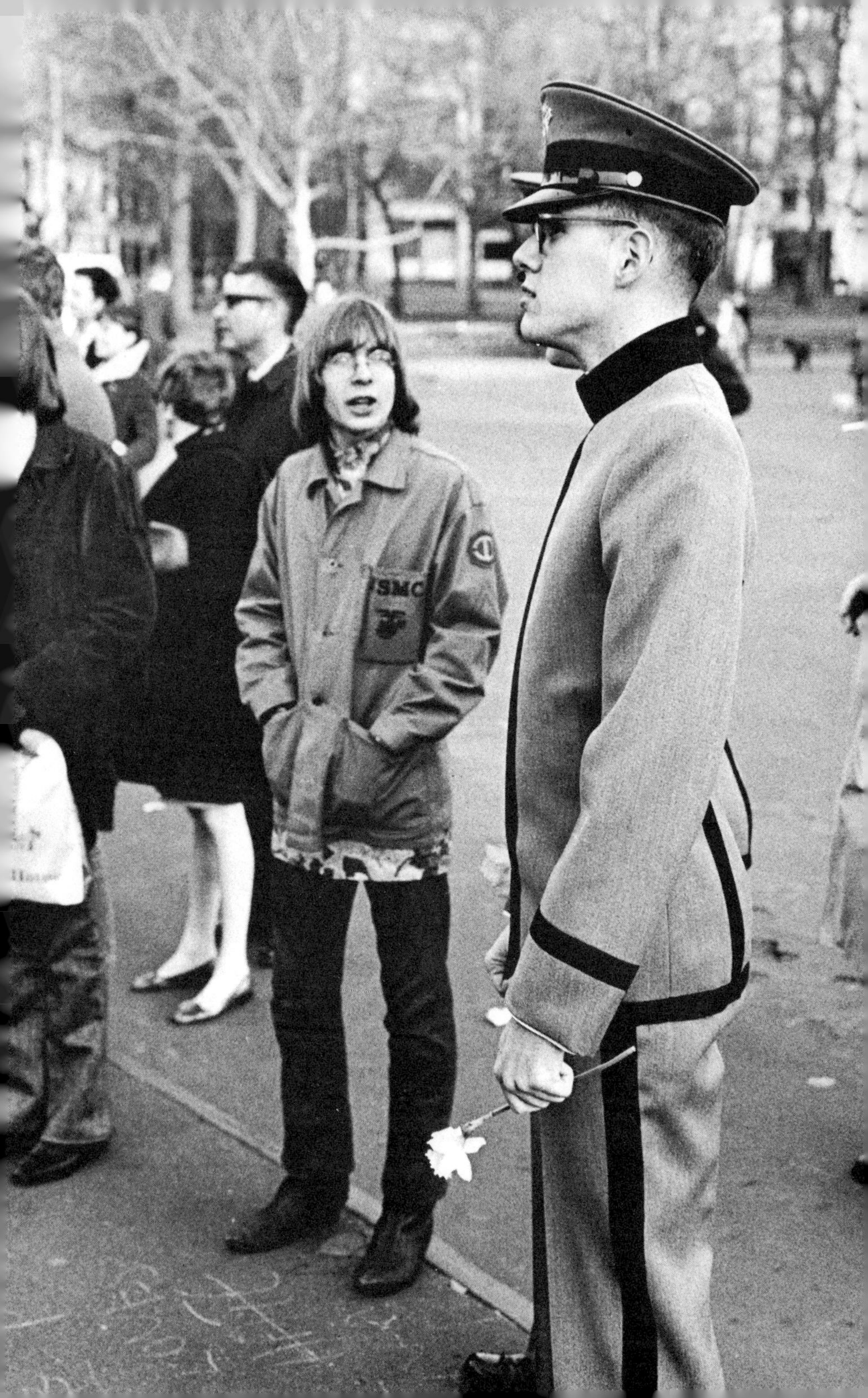
USMC

An answer

My friend McCormick
thinks he has an answer
to all the violence
in movies and on television.
"You sell licenses to producers
of movie and television shows.
They'd be like a hunting permit.
You wouldn't be allowed
to kill anyone in a TV program
without first buying a license.
It would cost you $1,000
to kill one man,
$2,000 to kill a woman
and $5,000 if you wanted
to kill a child."

                    Art Buchwald

With wonderful deathless ditties
We build up the world's great cities,
   And out of a fabulous story
   We fashion an empire's glory:
One man with a dream, at pleasure,
   Shall go forth and conquer a crown;
And three with a new song's measure
   Can trample a kingdom down.

                Arthur O'Shaughnessy

The Nazi–Fascist movement

Adolf Hitler, the leader of the Nazi party,
built his movement around veterans of the war
who found no satisfactory niche in civilian life.
Mussolini had done the same.
Memories of the desperate comradeship
of the trenches,
where shared pains, joys, and dangers
bound men powerfully together,
haunted old soldiers whose civilian life
lacked all value and meaning.
Nazis and Fascists sought to create
a similar comradeship in peacetime
by demanding total subordination
of individual and group self-interest
to the service of the nation,
as defined by themselves.
Hitler also invented an enemy—the Jews—
upon whom to focus hate and blame
for all of Germany's difficulties and failures.

     William H. McNeill

If man does find
the solution for world peace
it will be
the most revolutionary reversal
of his record
we have ever known.

    George Marshall

The secret of military uniform

It came upon me freshly
how the secret of uniform
was to make a crowd solid,
dignified, impersonal:
to give it the singleness
and tautness
of an upstanding man.
This death's livery
which walled its bearers
from ordinary life,
was sign that they had sold
their wills and bodies
to the State:
and contracted themselves
into a service
not the less abject
for that its beginning
was voluntary.

    Lawrence of Arabia

Why live?

God has not done what I asked Him to do; I am resigned; (not at all, I am only waiting). Oh, how tiresome it is to wait, to do nothing but wait! . . . I despise men profoundly and from conviction. I expect nothing good from them. . . . Those who are good are stupid, and those who are intelligent are either too false or too self-conceited. . . . The day will doubtless come when I shall think I have found a man, but if so, I shall deceive myself woefully. I can very well foresee that day; I shall then be blind. . . . Why live? since there is nothing but meanness and wickedness in the world? Why? Because I am reconciled to the knowledge that that is so; because, whatever people may say, life is very beautiful.

Is it not strange to hear me reason in this way? Yes, but this manner of reasoning in a young creature like me is but another proof of how bad the world is; it must be thoroughly saturated with wickedness to have so saddened me in so short a time. I am only fifteen.

Marie Bashkirtseff
Diary

The idea of enemies

From fifteen on you can think about enemies,
quite certainly think about enemies.
The idea of enemies is awful
it makes one stop remembering eternity
and the fear of death.
That is what enemies are.
Possessions are the same as enemies
only less so,
they too make one forget
eternity and the fear of death.

       Gertrude Stein

A young man must not sleep; his years are war . . .
       Robinson Jeffers

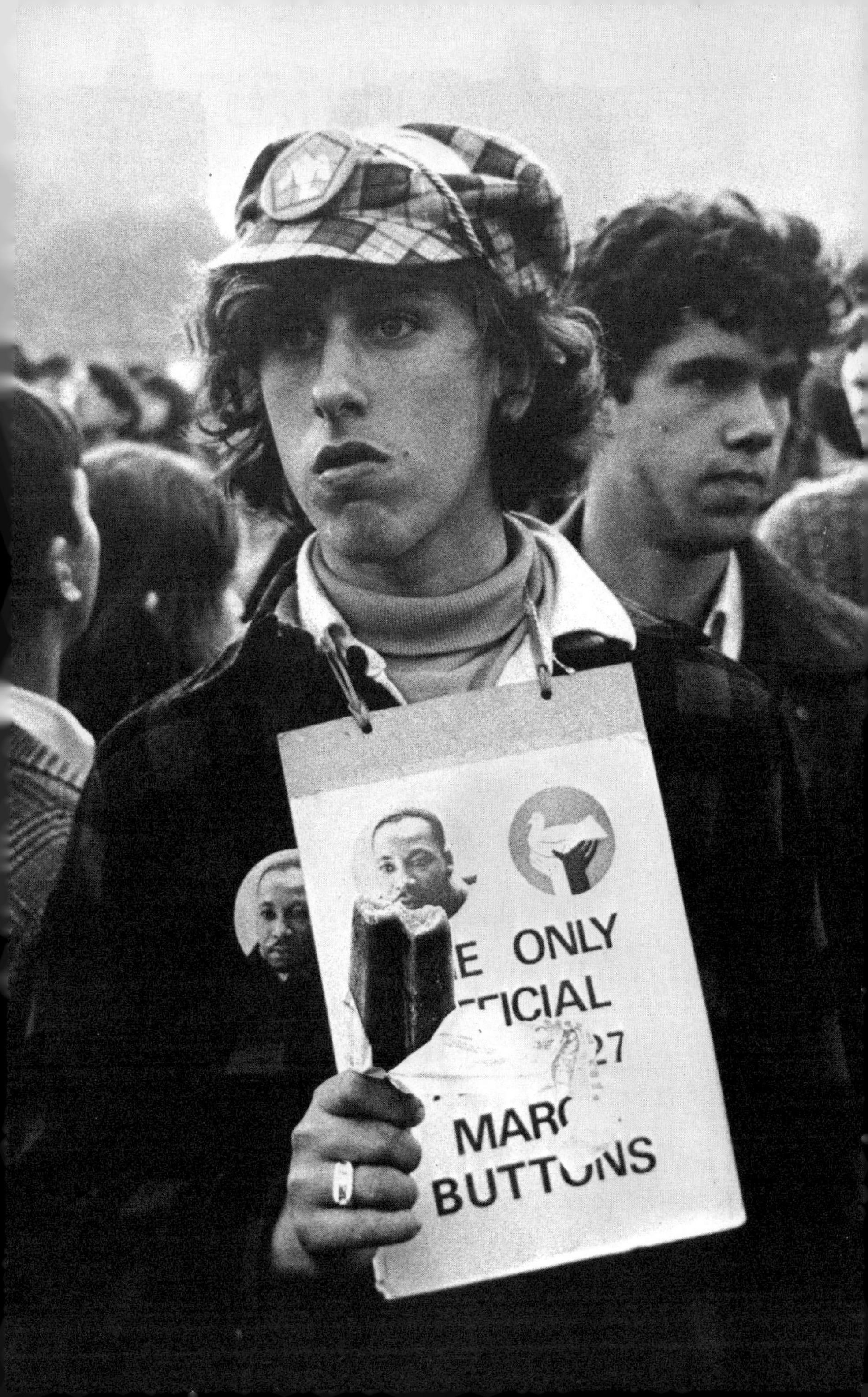
ONLY
BUTTONS

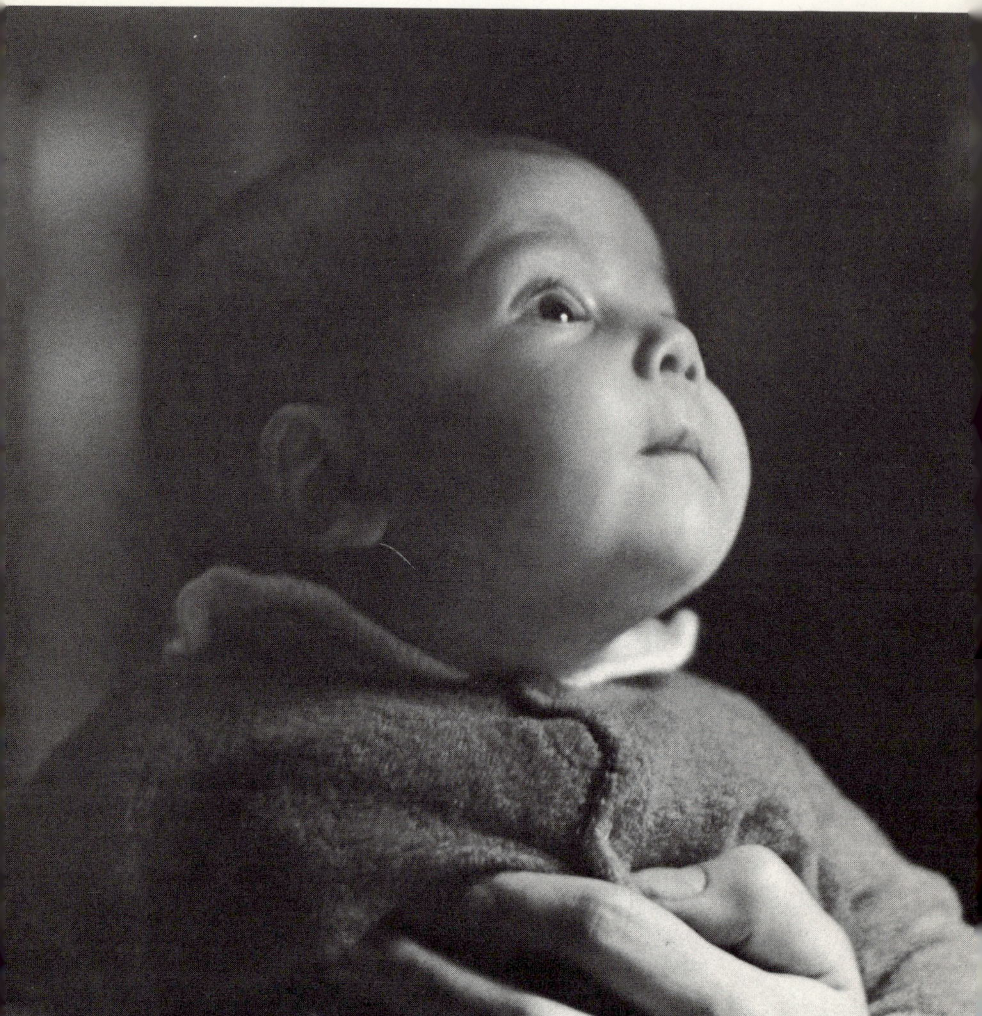

I am sick
and tired
of war.
Its glory
is all moonshine.
It is only those
who have never
fired a shot,
nor heard
the shrieks and groans
of the wounded,
who cry aloud for blood,
more vengeance,
more desolation.

War is hell.

> William Tecumseh Sherman
> Civil War general

War is unhealthy for children
and other living things.

> Graffito

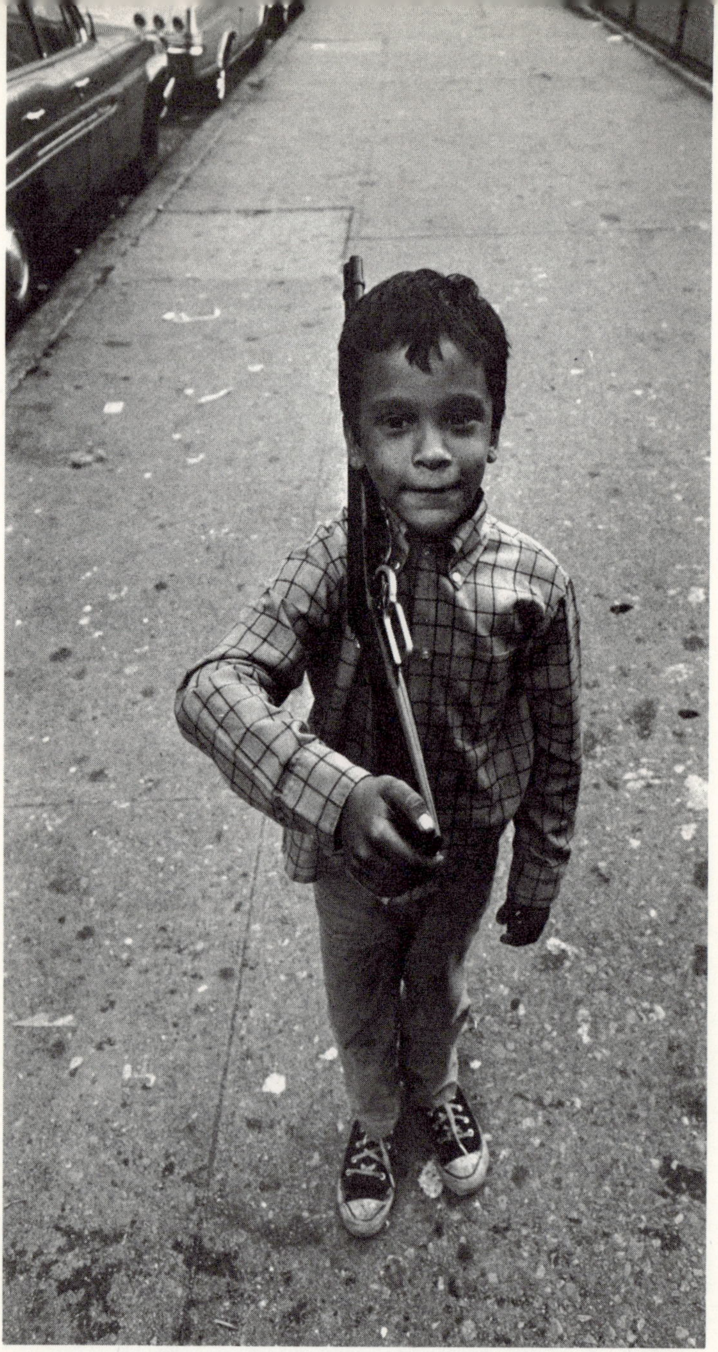

I hear the sound of the trumpet

My anguish, my anguish; I writhe in pain!
Oh, the walls of my heart!
My heart is beating wildly;
I cannot keep silent;
for I hear the sound of the trumpet,
the alarm of war.
Disaster follows hard on disaster,
the whole land is laid waste.
Suddenly my tents are destroyed,
my curtains in a moment.
How long must I see the standard,
and hear the sound of the trumpet?

                Jeremiah 4: 19–21

Maybe

Maybe
the "good life"
has to be postponed
till the killing stops—
for how can I claim
my own life to be
(let alone be good)
when my brothers' lives
are being claimed
as casualties—
worse, as victories?

                Corita Kent

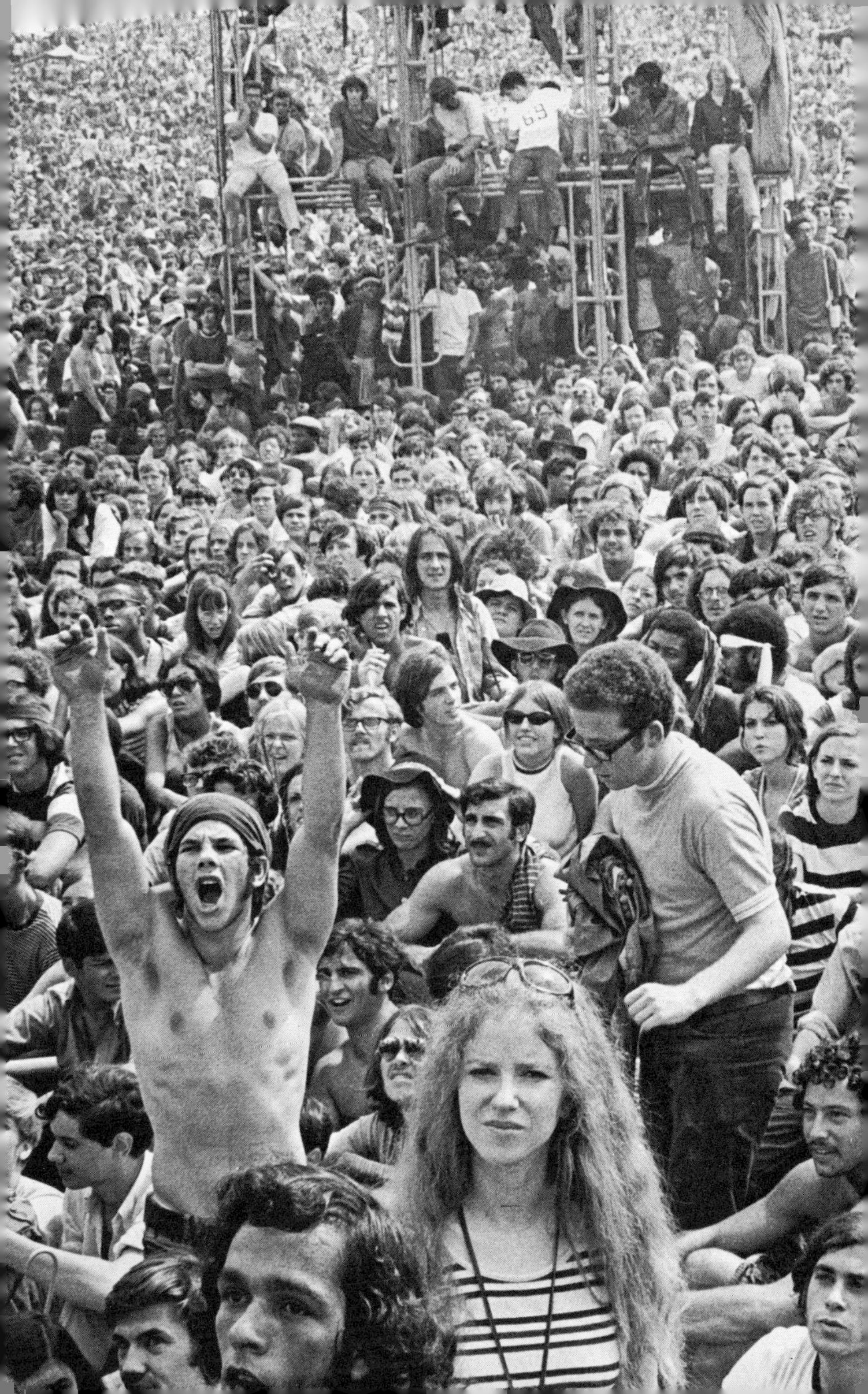

The sustaining illusion

In our activity alone do we find
the sustaining illusion
of an independent existence,
as against the whole scheme of things,
of which we form a helpless part.

Joseph Conrad
Nostromo

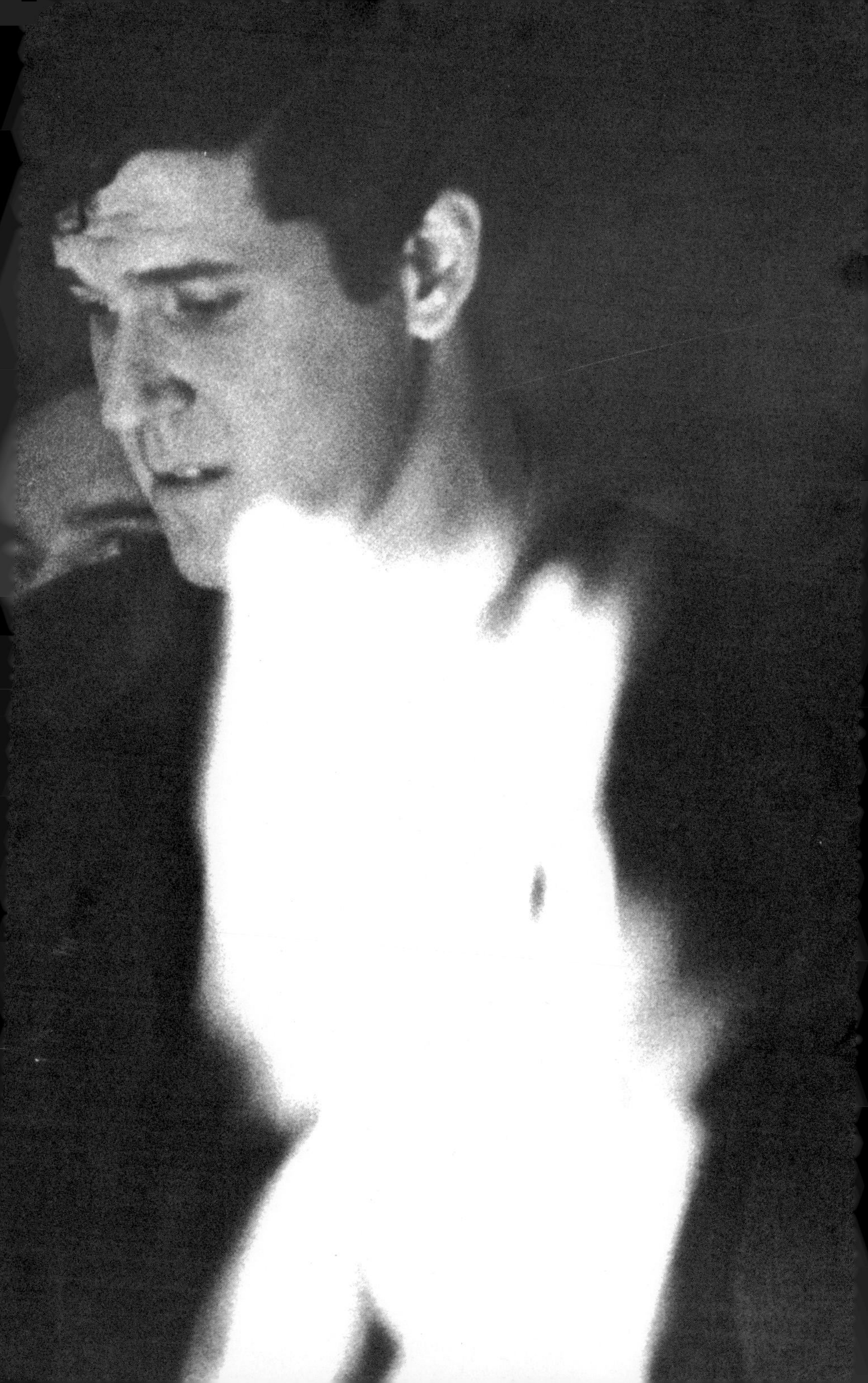

5

REVOLUTION

Throughout history, whenever a people is put under inescapable pressure, their emotions come to a boiling point and erupt. Anger spills over into activity and response. People get fed up, they can't take the oppression any longer. Workingmen unite, students unite, the underprivileged unite, even men in prison unite, they all demand their rights. Revolution will come inevitably; if not peacefully, then violently. What do people seem to be searching for deep down? Liberty? Love? Peace? A better world? But is it the desire for a better world that gives birth to revolution? Doesn't violence beget violence? And isn't human blood still human blood, whether it is the blood of patriots or tyrants? Do those who fight for freedom end by destroying freedom?

Those who make peaceful revolutions impossible
make violent revolutions inevitable.

John F. Kennedy

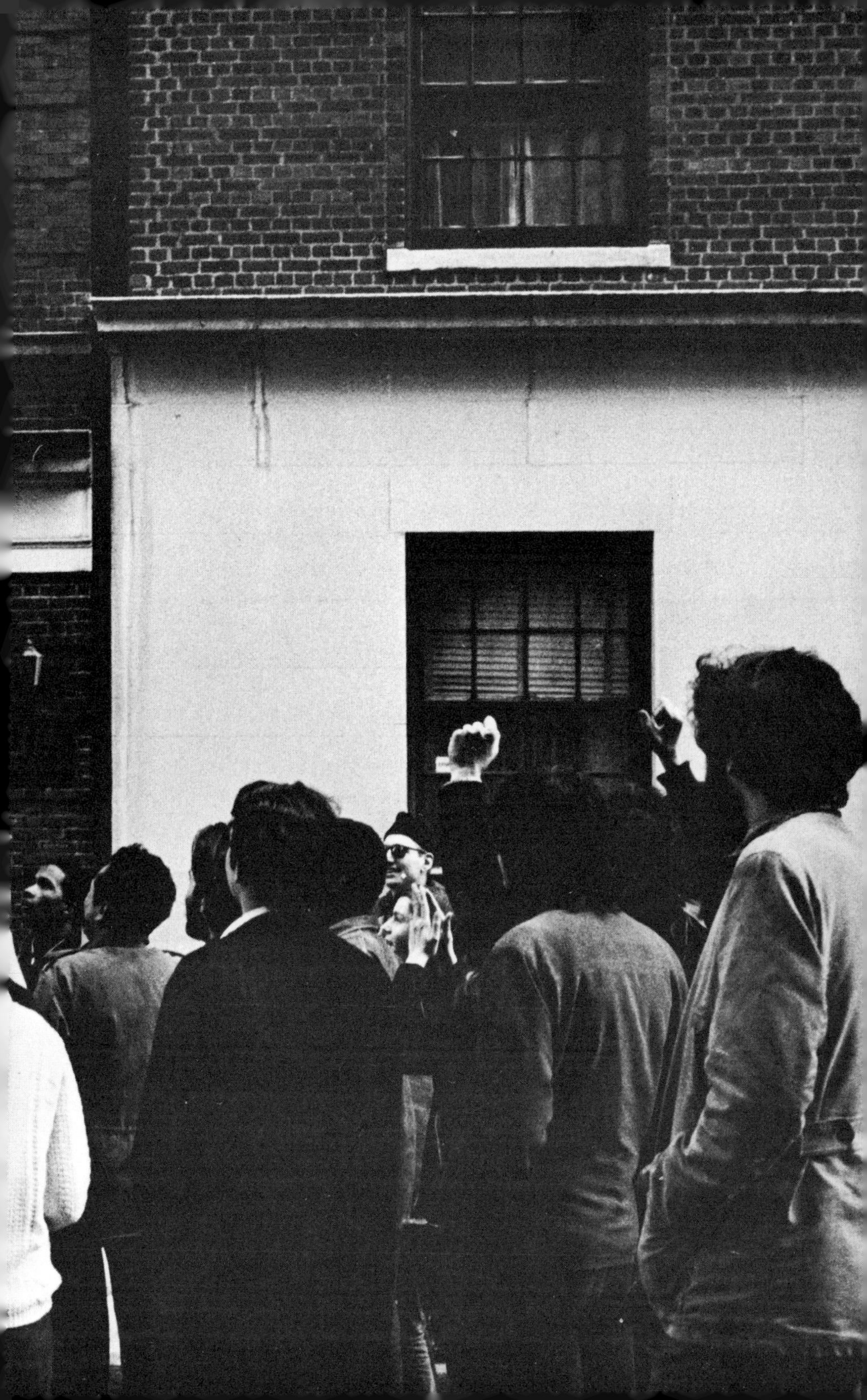

What Do We Do with Our Lives?

It was not the march of five years ago, it was frightening. Is it because things have changed since the days of the first Washington march? No. The hatred and bitterness you saw are there because things are essentially the same. God, they are worse. What happens to a human being who is once full of hope and confidence that he can make his presence felt in the world in a useful and healthy way? What happens when he is scorned and criticized and laughed at? We marched. O God, how we marched and sang and tried to turn from death to life.

We made mistakes. Sometimes we were rash and arrogant, but it was to push away the overwhelmingly helpless and insignificant feelings. We felt horror and grief and rage. We wanted to shake President Johnson and tell him to stop! stop! And the more we spoke out and marched and felt horror, the more the killing grew. Finally, a few more people joined in the protests and we were no longer cowards or traitors. But we were still helpless. We were drafted and trained to kill and sent to a very far away place to die. And our parents watched their children go to this insanity and did not seem to mind. Even when we came back in boxes.

We watched our cities crumbling and dying. We saw people of black and brown and red being denied their humanity. We went to the South and cried out to the Government for help and got nothing. A little here and there, but mostly it amounted to nothing. And we died there too.

We watched men whom we loved and had hope in (though they were not saints and were tainted with inhumanity as we all are) shot and buried.

An election approached and we once again had hope. He was no saint, but we worked our hearts out for him and had them broken. And hardened. At Chicago we grew up and felt our youth withering. Whom to turn to? Most of the people in the nation approved of the beating we received.

Nixon had a chance and he did not act. The Viet Nam War is not being ended. The cities are still dying; much of the countryside is dead. The "defense" budgets for the major countries of this earth are staggering, criminal.

"The System"—does it work? To some extent, yes. But not enough, not quickly enough. What are we supposed to do with our lives? How do we go about solving the complex problems of our world? "Work with the System," we hear. "You're young and strong, and besides, the problems aren't really as bad as you think."

There comes a time when pure frustration builds and breaks out and is ugly. You throw a bottle and it feels good. You say, "F---!" and it feels good. If you can't change it, blow it up. It becomes a very personal and illogical thing. Cops hate the damn Commie kids and the kids hate the damn pigs. We feel horror at death and find ourselves planning it in Weatherman basements. You say America is better than other places in the world. It is better than most, but, brother, it's nothing to be proud of, and it's getting worse each day.

Violence? I abhor it. Somehow throughout all the broken promises and worthless agreements and "reforms," I still abhor it and condemn it. We cannot change this world through violence—we can only end it. But I wonder if people will work in any other way. The young people—my brothers—I see them growing ugly and irrational and I hear them saying things that are not different from Johnson's words and justifications about Viet Nam. Our parents hate us, our politicians desert us, our hopes simply grew old and died.

I sound as though I am wallowing in self-pity because the world is too harsh. I'm not. I am only very tired.

Linda Eldredge

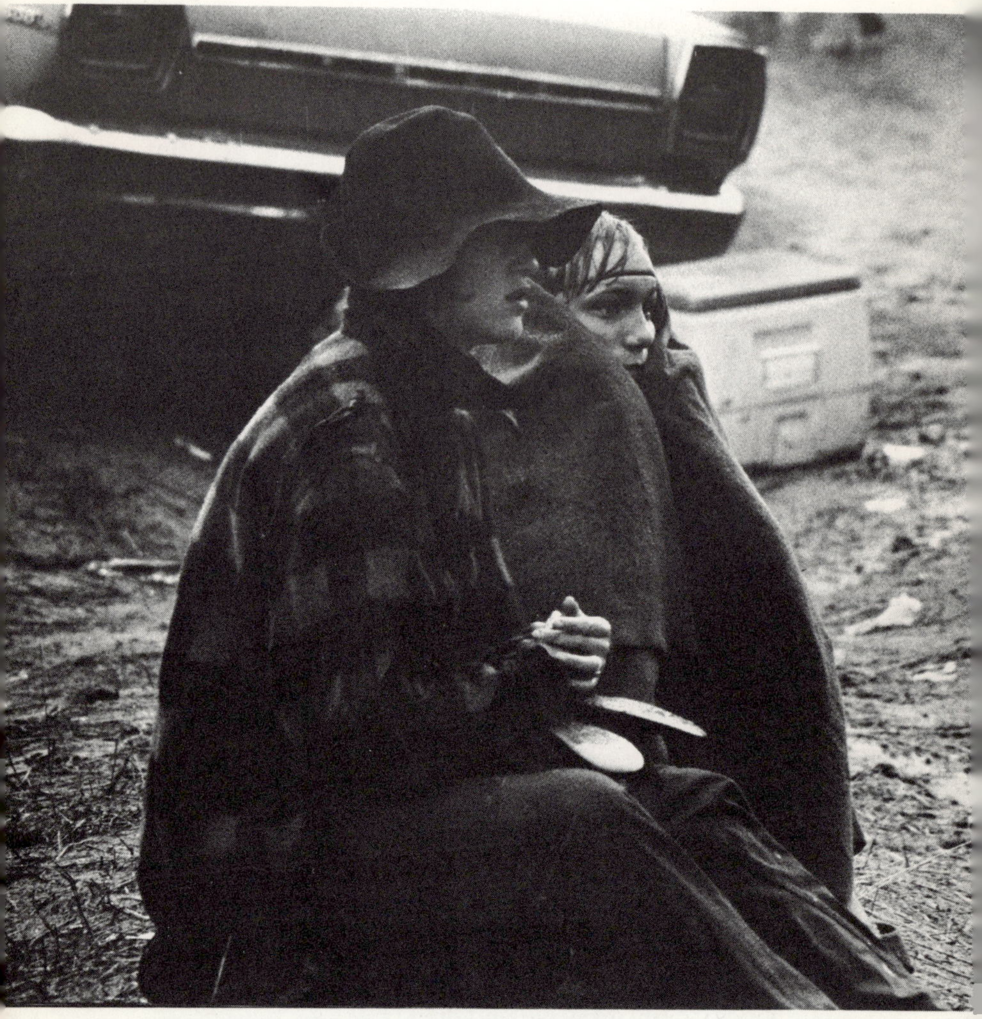

For Peter's grown
An' Paul's grown
An' Mary's grown
An' the times've grown.

Bob Dylan

A little rebellion

I hold it,
that a little rebellion,
now and then,
is a good thing,
and as necessary
in the political world
as storms in the physical. . . .
What country before
ever existed
a century and a half
without a rebellion? . . .
The tree of liberty
must be refreshed
from time to time
with the blood
of patriots and tyrants.
It is its natural manure.

              Thomas Jefferson

A world to win

The Communists disdain
to conceal
their views and aims.
They openly declare
that their ends
can be attained only
by the forcible overthrow
of all existing social conditions.
Let the ruling classes tremble
at a Communist revolution.
The proletarians
have nothing to lose
but their chains.
They have a world to win.
Workingmen of all countries, unite!

             The Communist Manifesto

The future of man

I sometimes fear
that creatures on other planets,
having achieved control of nature
but lacking an overriding devotion to life,
ended by using their control of nature
to destroy their life.
In this regard,
the future of man
remains profoundly uncertain.

                    Kenneth Keniston

Into the future

As long as man lives,
he is never content with the present,
but his intentions, his expectations,
his hopes, and his fears
are always stretched into the future . . .
The genuine life of man
is always before him;
it is always to be apprehended,
to be realized.
Man is always on the way;
each present hour is questioned
and challenged by its future.
That means at the same time
that the real essence
of all that man does
and undertakes in his present
becomes revealed only in the future
as important or vain,
as fulfillment or failure.
All actions are risks.

                    Rudolf Bultmann

We have done everything

Let us not, I beseech you, sir,
deceive ourselves longer.
Sir, we have done everything that could be done.
We have petitioned;
we have remonstrated;
we have supplicated;
we have prostrated ourselves before the throne
and have implored its interposition.
Our petitions have been slighted;
our remonstrances have produced
additional violence and insult;
our supplications have been disregarded;
and we have been spurned with contempt
from the foot of the throne.
In vain, after these things,
may we indulge the fond hope
of peace and reconciliation.
There is no longer any room for hope.

                            Patrick Henry

A violation of law

Isn't it singular that no one
ever goes to jail for waging wars,
let alone advocating them?
But the jails are filled
with those who want peace.
Not to kill is to be a criminal.
They put you right into jail
if all you do is ask them
to leave you alone.
Exercising the right to live
is a violation of law.
It strikes me as quite singular.

                    James Simon Kunen

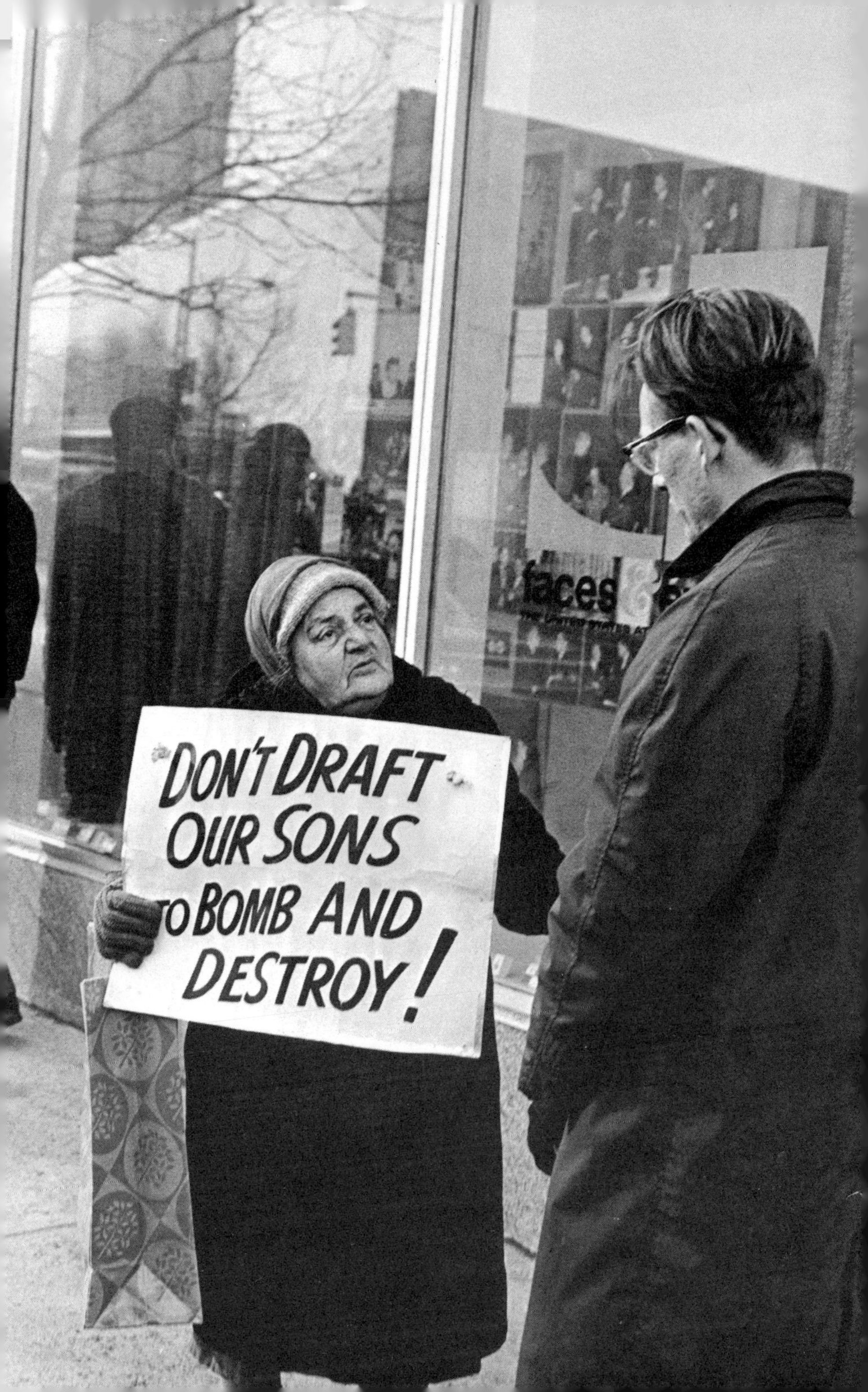
DON'T DRAFT
OUR SONS
to BOMB AND
DESTROY!
faces

A revolutionary

He said he was a revolutionary,
ready to kill or be killed for his cause,
for his ideology.
He was prepared to kill
for the sake of a better world.
To destroy the present social order
would of course produce more chaos,
but this confusion could be used
to build a classless society.
What did it matter if you destroyed some or many
in the process of building a perfect social order?
What mattered was not the present man,
but the future man;
the new world that they were going to build
would have no inequality,
there would be work for all,
and there would be happiness.

> Krishnamurti

Put your finger on a pacifist,
and you put your finger
on some degree of anarchism.

> Bayard Rustin

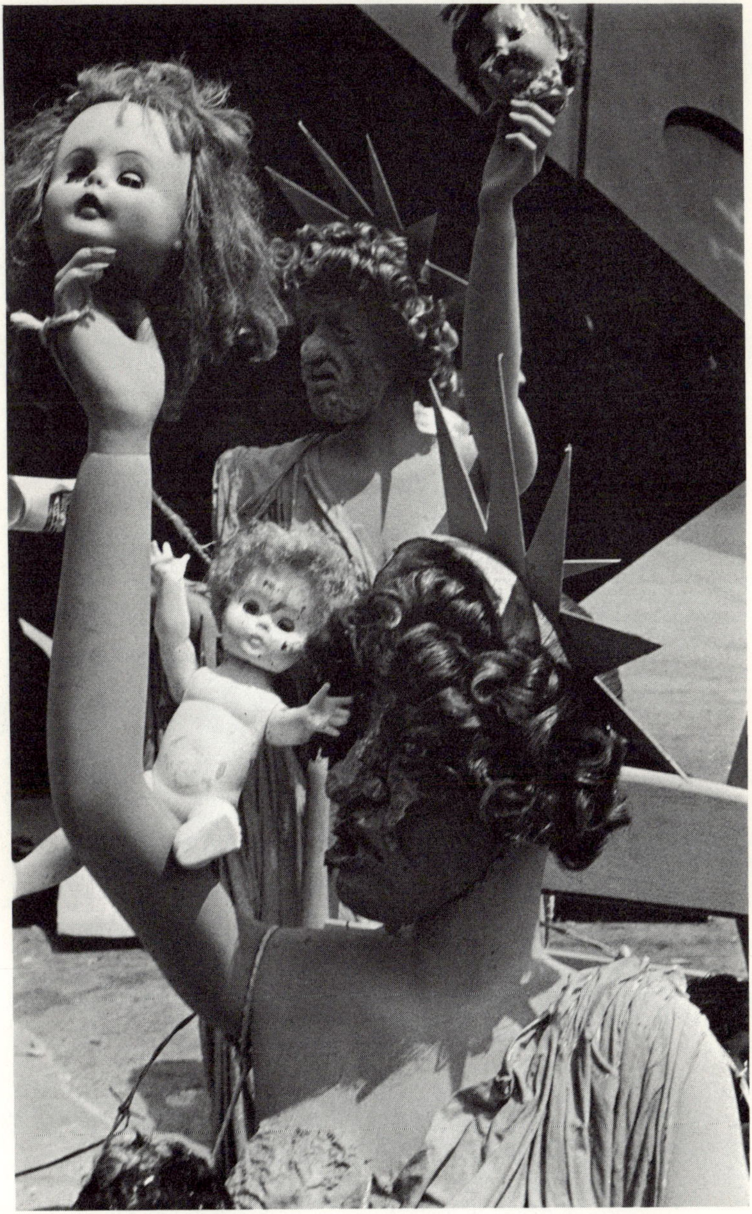

Violent revolution

It is clear
that the liberation
of the oppressed class
is impossible
without a violent revolution,
and without the destruction
of the machinery
of State power,
which has been created
by the governing class
and in which
this "separation" is embodied.

> Nikolai Lenin

Whenever men organize to fight for freedom, they end by destroying freedom.

> Jack Schwartzman

How far can one bend
and still call himself a man?

Tom Gardner

Laws of violence

The first law of violence is continuity.
Once you start using violence,
you cannot get away from it. . . .
The second law is reciprocity. . . .
violence creates violence,
begets and creates violence. . . .
The third law is sameness. . . .
It is impossible to distinguish
between justified and unjustified violence,
between violence that liberates
and violence that enslaves. . . .
All kinds of violence are the same.
Violence begets violence—*nothing else*.
This is the fourth law of violence.

                              Jacques Ellul

A point of absurdity

Inevitably there will be more and more people
demanding more and not getting it;
and therefore there will be
more and more shortness of temper
and eventual violence.
And the violence is going to be
stupid violence.
If the immolation of a boy with gasoline
in front of the United Nations building
isn't considered significant,
it's terrible.
When a man sacrifices his life
and it doesn't have any significance for us,
when it just seems like a steal
from somebody else's act,
we are reaching a point of absurdity
in our reactions.

Gerald Sykes

A land of plenty

The Utopians speak of a day
when there will be no police.
There will be nothing for them to do.
Every man will do his duty,
will respect the rights
of his neighbor,
will not disturb the peace.
The needs of all
will be taken care of.
Everyone will have sympathy
for his fellow man.
There will be no such thing as crime.
There will be, of course, no prisons.
No electric chairs, no gas chambers.
The hangman's rope will be
the thing of the past.
The entire earth
will be a land of plenty.
There will be no crimes
against property,
no speculation.

It is easy to see that we are
not on the verge of entering Utopia:
there are cops everywhere.

      Eldridge Cleaver

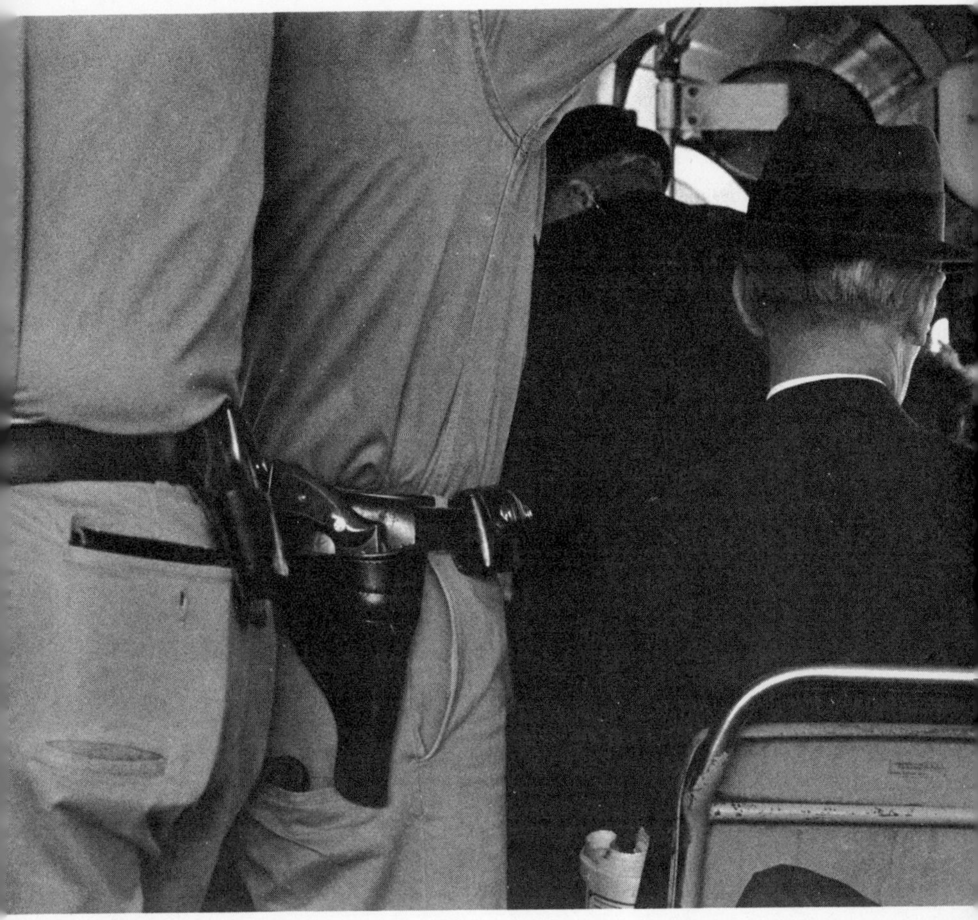

Disobedience to bad laws

Dramatic disobedience to the law
by a minority
may be the only effective way
of catching the attention
or winning the support
of the majority.
Most classic cases of civil disobedience,
from the early Christians to Gandhi,
exemplify this truth.
Civil disobedience,
like almost no other technique,
can shame a majority
and make it ask itself
just how far it is willing to go . . .
Disobedience to bad laws
can sometimes jolt democratic processes
into motion.

                        Charles Frankel

Violent protest

I believe this Administration finds itself today embracing a philosophy which appears to lack appropriate concern for the attitude of a great mass of Americans—our young people...

Today, our young people, or at least a vast segment of them, believe they have no opportunity to communicate with Government, regardless of Administration, other than through violent confrontation. But I am convinced we—and they—have the capacity, if we will have the willingness, to learn from history.

About 200 years ago there was emerging a great nation in the British Empire, and it found itself with a colony in violent protest by its youth—men such as Patrick Henry, Thomas Jefferson, Madison and Monroe, to name a few. Their protests fell on deaf ears, and finally led to war. The outcome is history. If we read history, it clearly shows that youth in its protest must be heard. Let us show them we can solve our problems in an enlightened and positive manner...

Walter J. Hickel
in a letter to Richard M. Nixon

6

RATIONAL ANALYSIS

There are those who evaluate war from the broad perspective of all mankind, reflecting on its causes and remedies. They are the philosophers, sociologists, and scientists—like Plato, Freud, Huxley, Andreski, Wright, and Eastman—who feel that man probably cannot live without aggression and the need to dominate. He cannot live without an "enemy." Perhaps, the thinkers suggest, the deeper need of human beings is to find unity and a common meaning, a cause in which they can spend their inexhaustible energies. Historically, war may be a most effective instrument in bringing people together and giving them a shared purpose. The question: Is there anything else, besides war, that can give mankind unity and purpose?

A dialogue with Socrates

And the country which was enough to support the original inhabitants will be too small now, and not enough?

Quite true.

Then a slice of our neighbors' land will be wanted by us for pasture and tillage, and they will want a slice of ours, if, like ourselves, they exceed the limit of necessity, and give themselves up to the unlimited accumulation of wealth?

That, Socrates, will be inevitable.

And so we shall go to war, Glaucon. Shall we not?

Most certainly, he replied.

Plato

They say

In some happy corners of the earth, they say, where nature brings forth abundantly whatever man desires, there flourish races whose lives go gently by, unknowing of aggression or constraint. This I can hardly credit; I would like further details about these happy people.

Sigmund Freud
in a letter to Albert Einstein

The use of force

On the surface there tends
to be an abhorrence
of force, coercion:
Human liberty
is being trampled upon.
Yet, with so much emphasis
and support for human rights
on one hand,
and condemnation of violence
on the other,
one can justly ask
"Can human rights
be defended
without recourse
to the use of force?"

                Thomas J. O'Connor

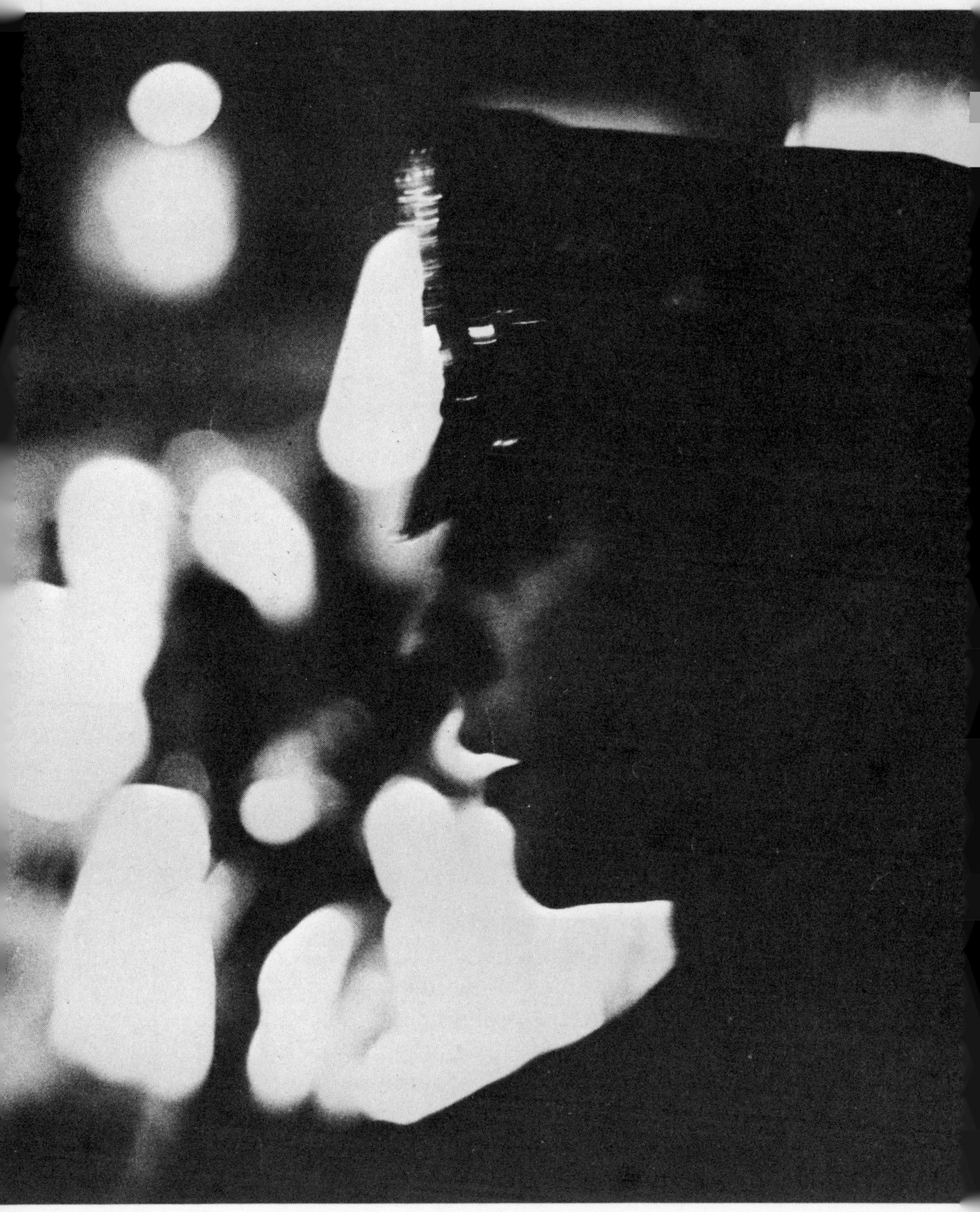

Without war

It is an unpleasant truth
that, human nature being what it is,
without war
civilization would still be divided
into small bands wandering
in the forests and jungles.

    Stanislav Andreski

I have never met anybody
who wasn't against war.
Even Hitler and Mussolini were,
according to themselves.

    David Low

Not with my life you don't.

Pentagon wall graffito

"I believe we should get the war over," I said.
"It would not finish if one side stopped fighting.
It would only be worse if we stopped fighting."

"It could not be worse,"
Passini said respectfully.
"There is nothing worse than war."

"Defeat is worse."

Ernest Hemingway
A Farewell to Arms

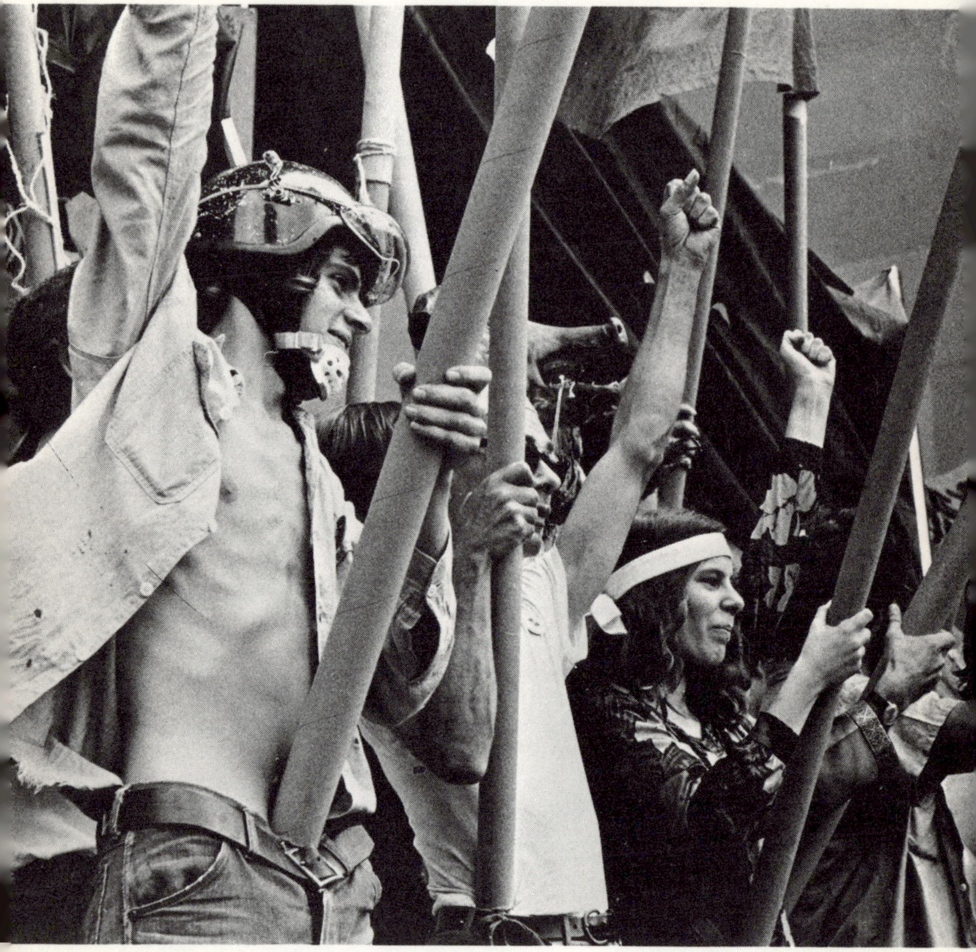

A widespread characteristic

A dominance drive
is probably
a widespread characteristic
of higher animals,
but fighting for dominance
is less characteristic
of animals in general
than of human beings.

                        Quincy Wright
                        A Study of War

We have abandoned
our first love,
human liberty,
and we are in love
with industrial efficiency
and the business prosperity
of the nation.

      Max Eastman (1928)

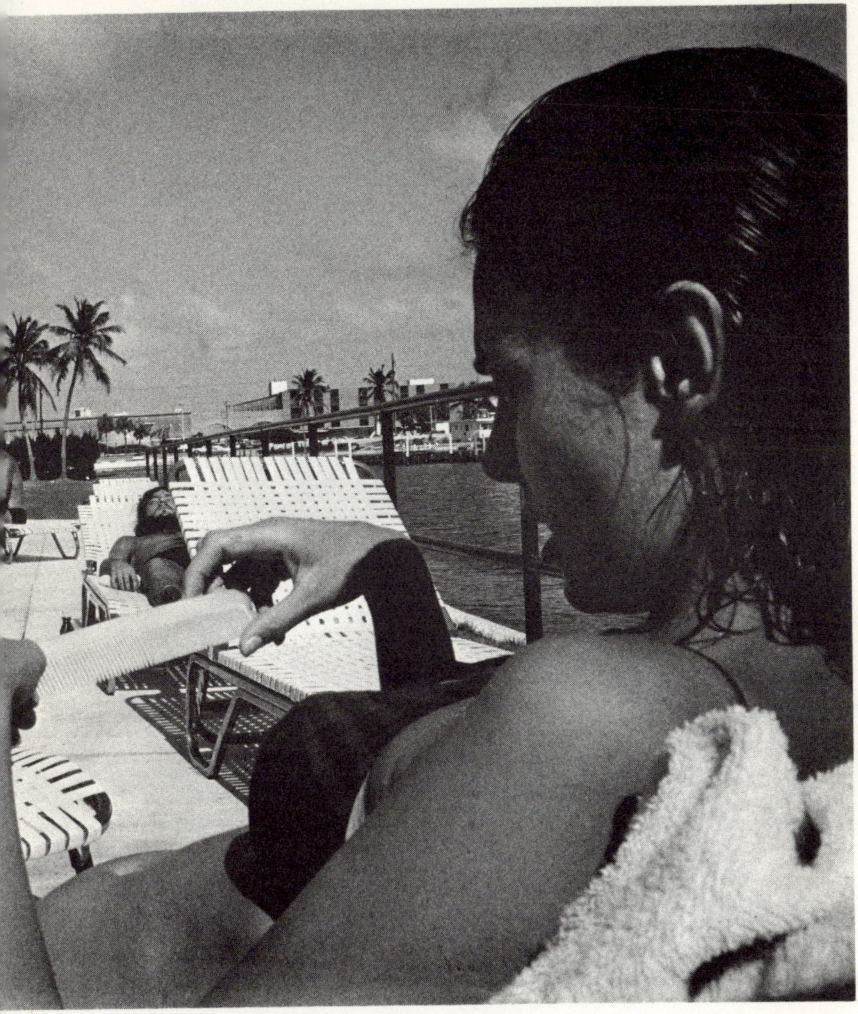

The grave problem

This is the grave problem:
that peoples do not have true pictures,
one of the other;
thus myths are born and nourished
and world understanding is put in jeopardy.

Lester Markel

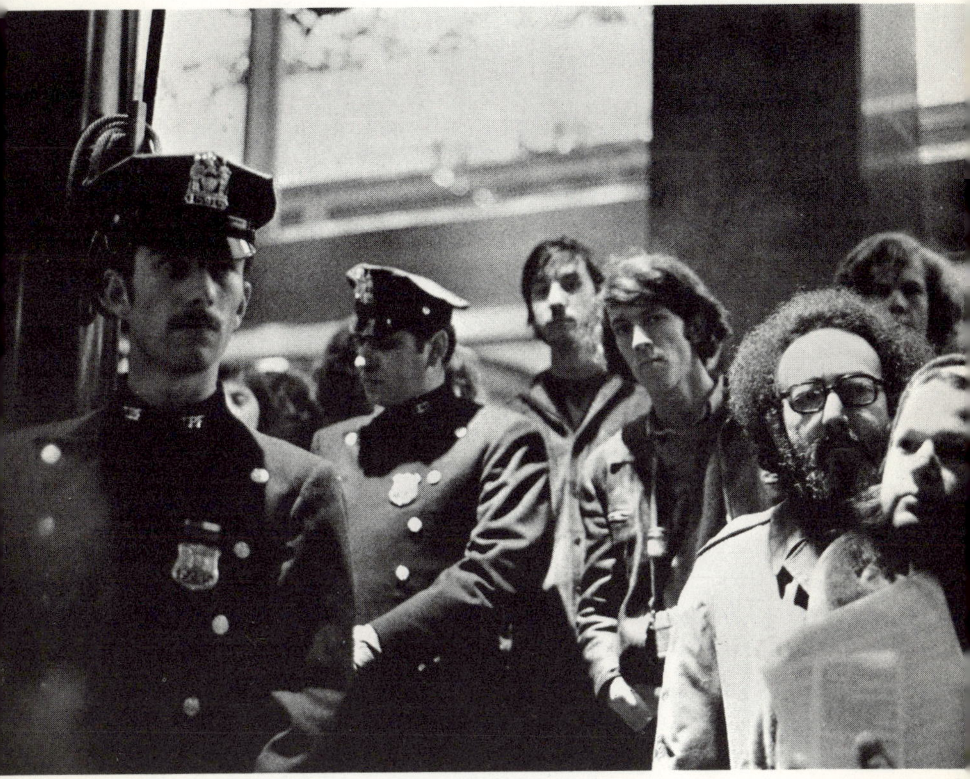

PART III

THE POSSIBILITY OF PEACE

Everyone wants peace. Religious leaders preach against evil and war. Industrialists and economists encourage a new order of peace and prosperity. Politicians promise that they will prevent war. Yet citizens are horrified to watch on television the killing of little children and the murder of innocent civilians. "Make love, not war," is chanted over and over again. Other voices say other things, in different contexts . . . and with different meanings. Everyone wants peace. The problem is that we don't have it.

Monuments of bronze and marble and sterile ceremonies on Memorial Day are the remnants of war. But what are the possibilities of peace? Where can one turn to find hope?

7

BEYOND NATIONALISM

The first stage in man's pilgrimage toward peace is to build bridges of understanding between nations and continents, to view all men from the single perspective of humanity. Mankind is one. Beauty, truth, and goodness are not mine or yours, but ours. Facing people who want peace is the challenge to create symbols of one world—like the acorns of Yoka Ono and John Lennon—and to nourish one spirit of brotherhood among all men, so that people see themselves, not as Americans or Frenchmen or Japanese, but as earthmen, all living and working within the framework of a single human destiny.

Don't touch my castle

They made castles of sand,
and each child defended his castle
and said, "This one is mine."
They kept their castles separate
and would not allow any mistakes
about which was whose.
When the castles were all finished,
one child kicked over someone else's castle
and completely destroyed it.
The owner of the castle flew into a rage,
pulled the other child's hair,
struck him with his fist and bawled out,
"He has spoilt my castle!
Come along all of you and help me
to punish him as he deserves."
The others all came to his help.
They beat the child with a stick
and then stamped on him
as he lay on the ground . . .
Then they went on playing in
their sand castles,
each saying, "This is mine,
no one else may have it.
Keep away! Don't touch my castle!"
But evening came;
it was getting dark and they all thought
they ought to be going home.
No one now cared what became of his castle.
One child stamped on his,
another pushed his over with both his hands.
Then they turned away and went back
each to his home.

       Yogacara Bhumi Sutra

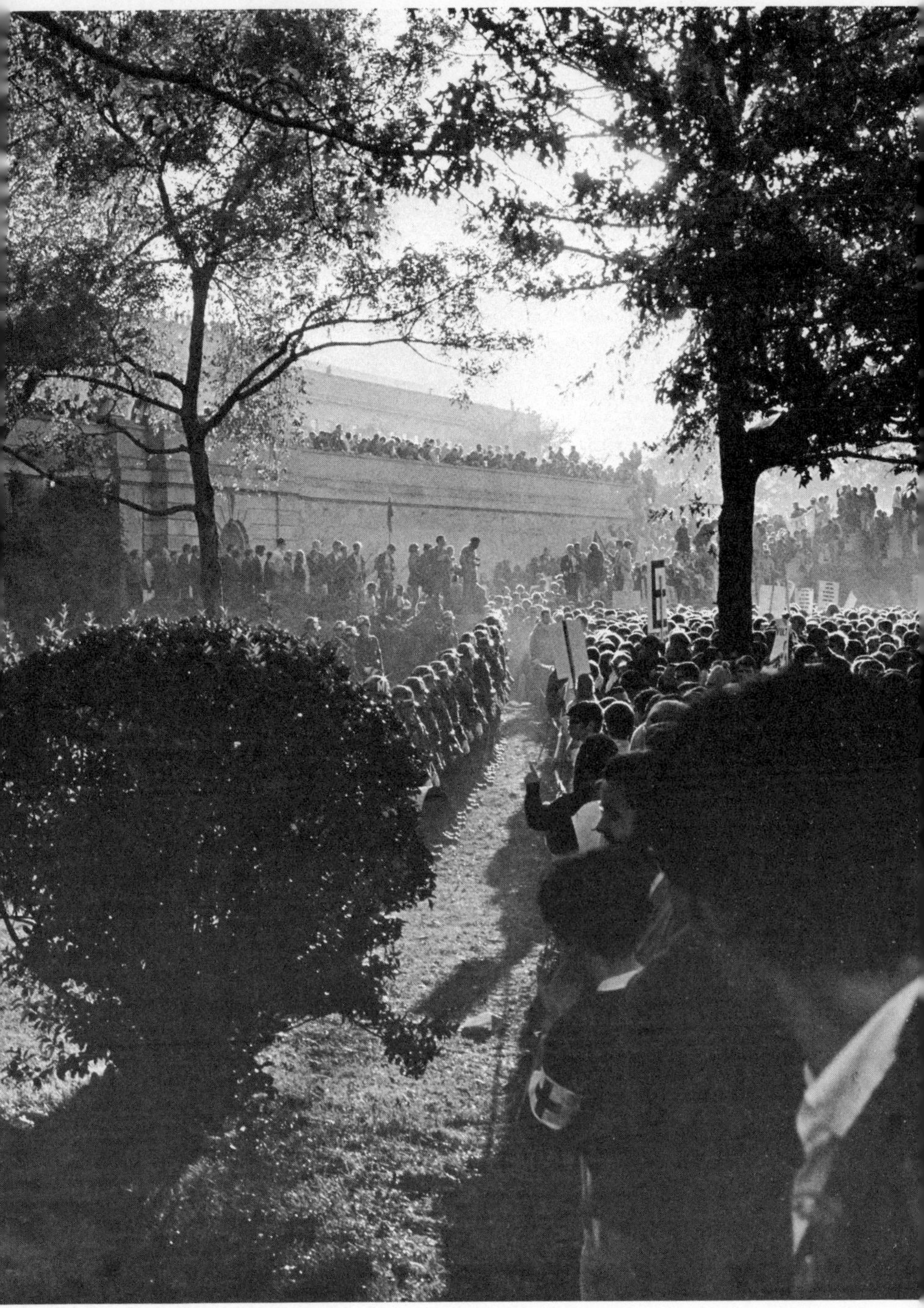

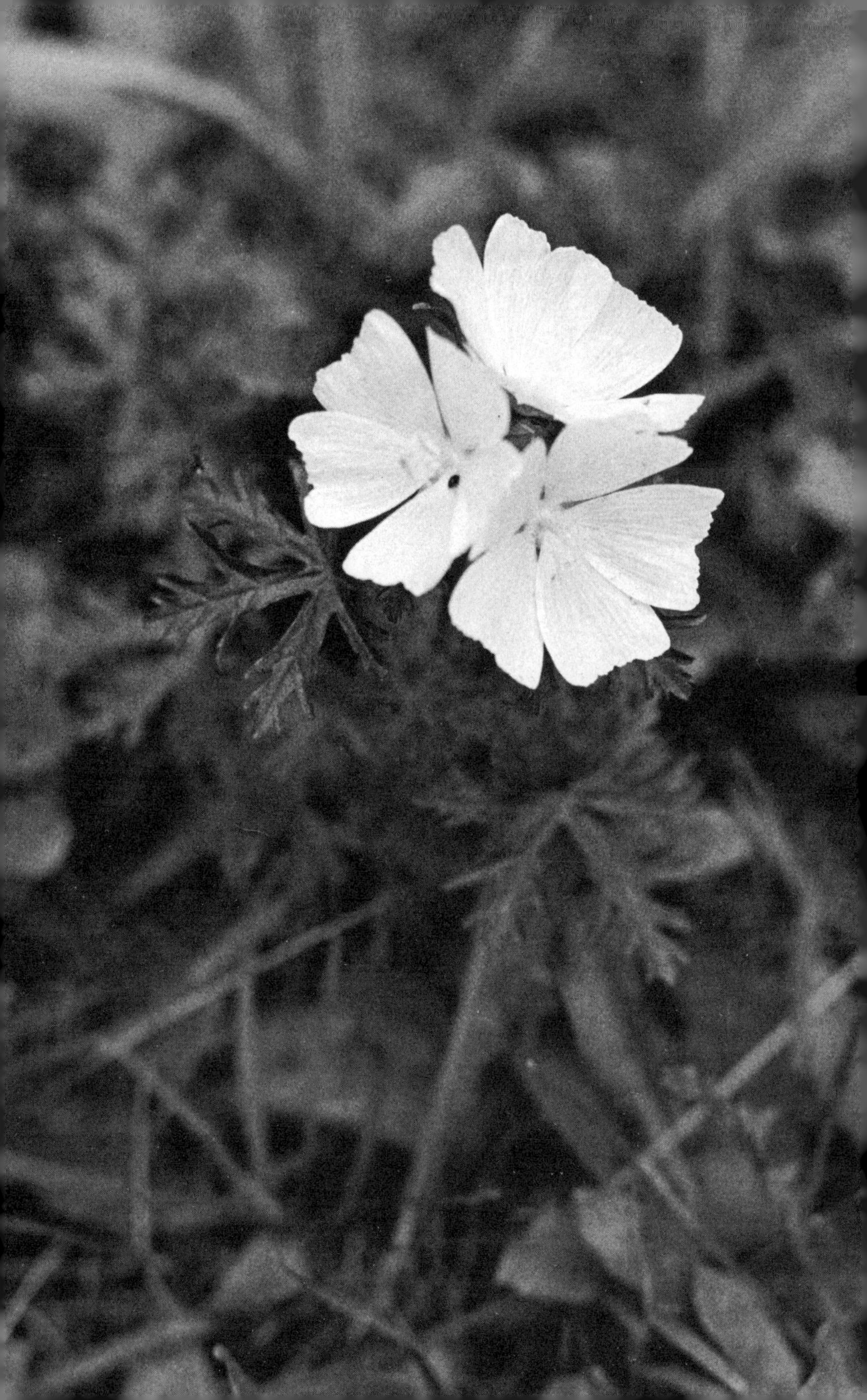

For peace

We're going to send two acorns for peace
to every world leader
from John and Yoko.
Perhaps if they plant them
and watch them grow
they may get the idea
into their heads.

                        John Lennon

Hope for all the world

The Declaration of Independence gave liberty
not alone to the people of this country,
but hope to all the world,
for all future time.
It was that which gave promise
that in due time the weights
would be lifted from the shoulders
of all men,
and that all should have an equal chance.
This is the sentiment embodied
in the Declaration of Independence . . .
I would rather be assassinated on this spot
than surrender it.

                        Abraham Lincoln

Symbols and traditions

Germans think of themselves as belonging to the land of Beethoven and Goethe; Norwegians preserve the relics of the Vikings and in fantasy share in their fabulous exploits; Greeks do not forget Praxiteles and Demosthenes. Flags, martial music, noble ruins are profoundly significant to the citizens whose security and whose self-esteem are inseparable from the tradition of his people.

Most symbols are of an exclusively parochial order. They mark off my country from yours, or they mark off my religion from yours, or my caste from yours. World symbols are virtually lacking: No world parks, gardens, universities, and few symbolic world-minded documents. There is no world currency, no genuine world capital. A few fine words have been spoken: The Atlantic Charter, the United Nations Charter, the Preamble to the UNESCO Charter. But these symbols are little known and still fail to rally appreciable loyalty. Just as the diversified egos within a nation cannot be fused into one "we" without the aid of tradition and symbol, so, too, international loyalty cannot be achieved without a common focus of thought and the common uplift that comes from symbols of transnational unity.

Gordon W. Allport

Happy endings

Americans are obsessed with happy endings.
Our novels, magazines, television programs,
are all devoted to the happy ending.
One has to criticize leadership
in this country
for playing up to this obsession,
for intimating that there is always
a path to a happy ending
for every problem.
There isn't any happy ending
to any of the present situations.
The ending will be intensely disagreeable
to Americans, because most of the endings
will call for vast changes
in the status quo,
and Americans simply don't want
to change the status quo.

      W. H. Ferry

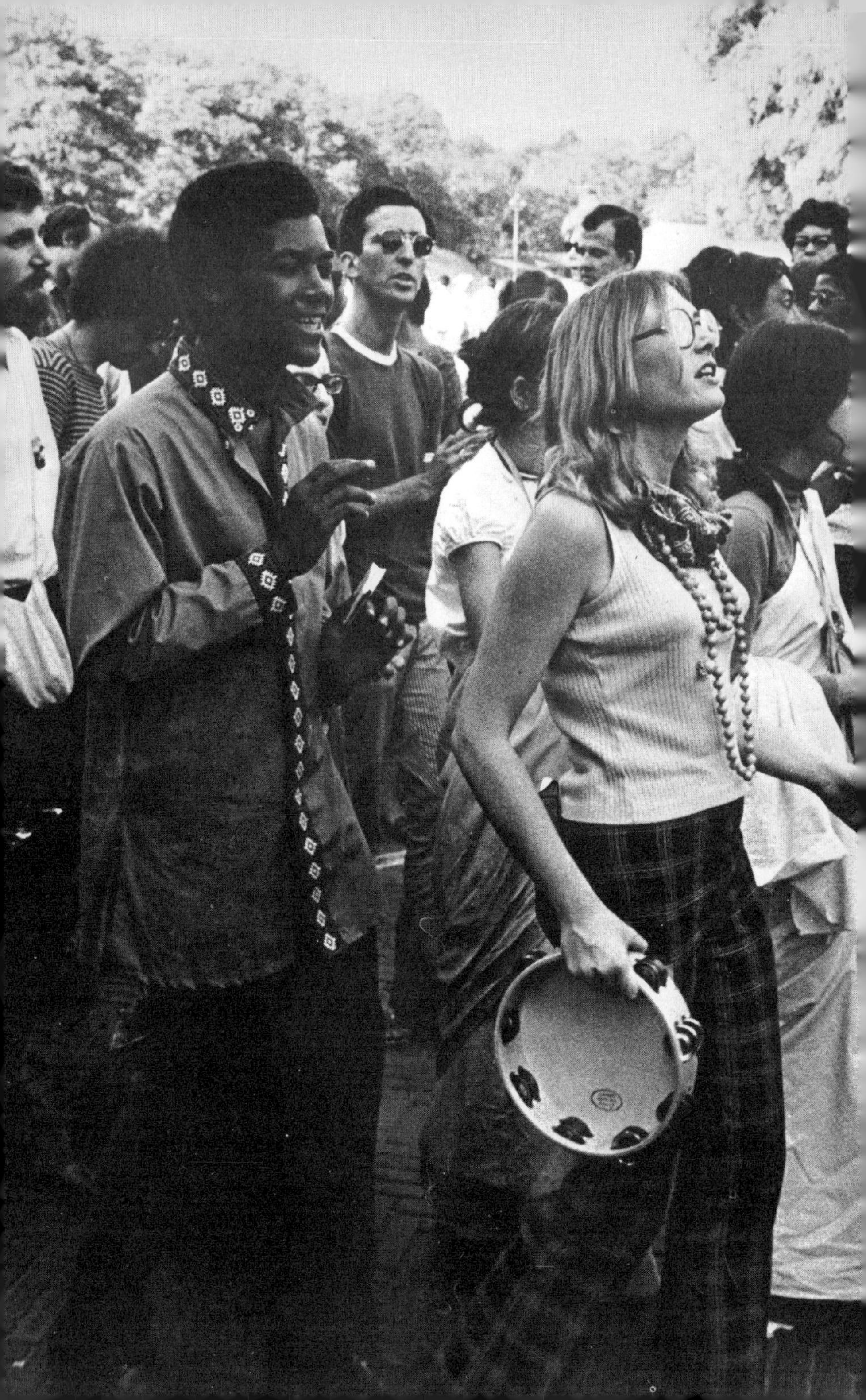

A spirit of brotherhood
Whereas recognition of the inherent dignity and of the equal and inalienable rights of all members of the human family is the foundation of freedom, justice and peace in the world,

Whereas disregard and contempt for human rights have resulted in barbarous acts which have outraged the conscience of mankind, and the advent of a world in which human beings shall enjoy freedom of speech and belief and freedom from fear and want has been proclaimed as the highest aspiration of the common people,

Whereas it is essential, if man is not to be compelled to have recourse, as a last resort, to rebellion against tyranny and oppression, that human rights should be protected by the rule of law ...

All human beings are born free and equal in dignity and rights. They are endowed with reason and conscience and should act towards one another in a spirit of brotherhood ...

>Universal Declaration of Human Rights (1948)

Better and better

America could take over the world.
It's true what they say.
But never by force.
All it will take
is pointing the energy of America
in the right direction,
like turning the wheel of an automobile.
And it's happening now with the kids.

Children of fourteen are able
to look at their older brothers and say,
"No, that's not the way.
With drugs and all that jumping about."
They've already looked at their parents
and they *know* that's not the way.
So each generation peels a little bit away.
We're cutting life down to a fine thing,
and it keeps getting better and better,
like a healing.

     Donovan Leitch

Wherever the standard
of freedom and independence
has been or shall be unfurled,
there will be America's heart . . .
But she does not go abroad
in search of monsters to destroy . . .
(If she did) the fundamental maxims
of her policy
would insensibly change
from liberty to force . . .
She might become
the dictatress of the world.
She would no longer
be the ruler of her own spirit.

     John Quincy Adams

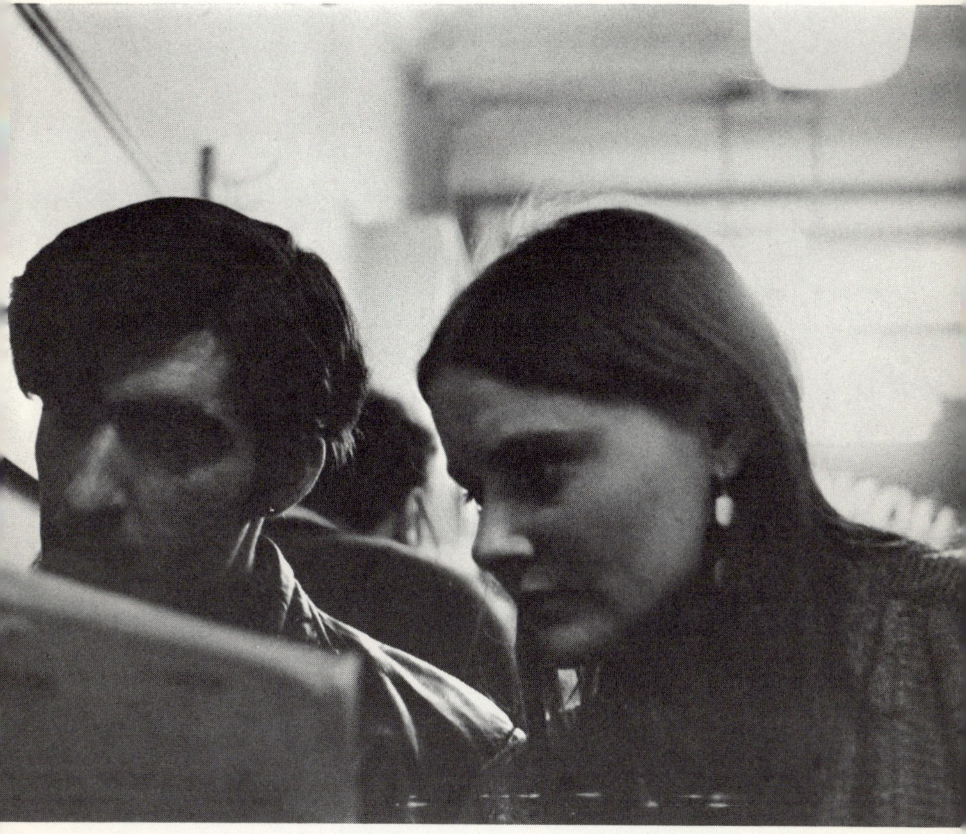

8
A NEW CONSCIOUSNESS

"Awareness is the new frontier," says Mason Williams. There is a need, in this search for a world of peace, for a freshness of vision, a need to stop the maddening pace, to slow the momentum of panic, to stop and turn around completely, to look long and hard, and think. A new mentality, a new awareness, a conversion from old ways of thinking, are demanded of the pioneers of peace. Fresh and startling revelations are at hand for those who can recognize them: antidotes for war and stagnation, for violence as well as apathy. In the new consciousness there are pathways to explore—of care, sensitivity to others, creativity, and love.

What kind of world?

Some people say, "We want a world
where people feel like people
and life is respected."
But at the same time
they are willing to blow up a building
or get someone else to blow it up
and destroy a few lives.
Something has gone haywire
in our thinking.
Living that way
you never get what you want.
You only get what you do.
You don't get what you talk about
or what you dream about.
You get what you've done
at the end of a day.

                              Joan Baez

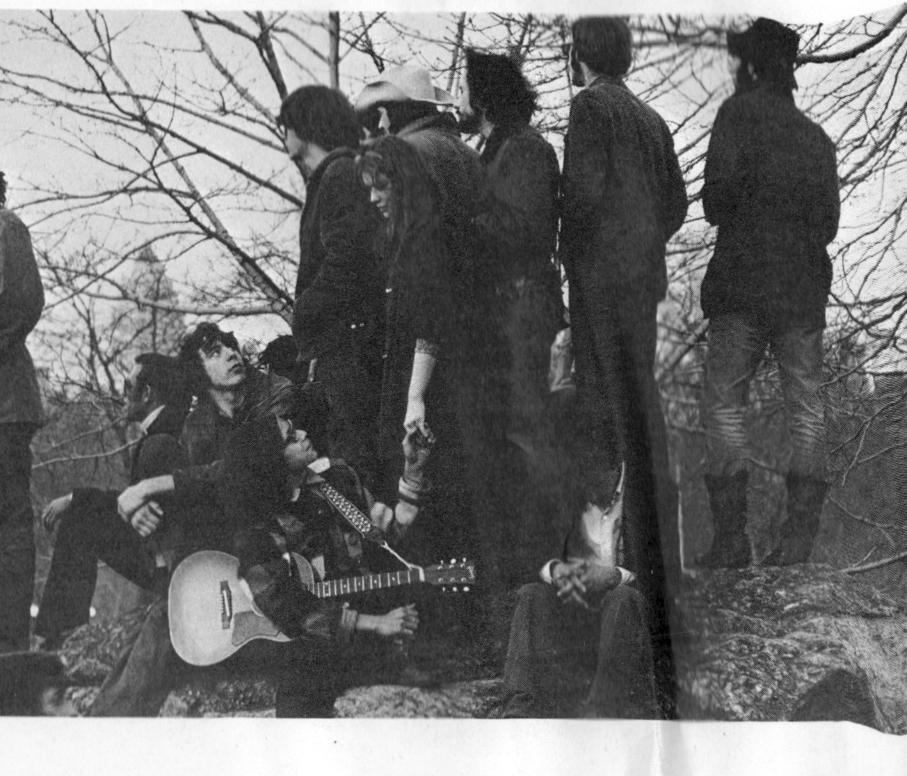

The best place

I just want to be left alone.
I'm tired of being threatened
and just want to live in peace.
Jail might be the only peaceful place around.
I remember when we used to play Monopoly
and somebody got all the houses and hotels
and was sucking money out of me
that the best place to be was jail.
Otherwise, I'd lose the game.

      Jeffrey Martens

Only to the extent that young people
are brought up differently
from their parents
can a society seriously hope
to fashion a world that is better.

      Eli Ginzberg

Revolution and conversion
have the same meaning:
to turn around completely.

   Denis de Rougemont

New toys

The scientists generally agree that the world will see the decline of nationalistic rivalries and the waning of ideological passions that today erupt into world tensions and bloodshed. They predict instead greater international co-operation.

But they are not predicting an end to the insanity of war. On the contrary, they foresee a fascinating array of new toys for the soldiers; disintegrator ray guns; acoustic shock waves; cheap, lightweight nuclear weapons that even gangsters can make; ocean-bed fortifications; and antigravity mechanisms that will give future GI's three-dimensional mobility. They even expect weather wars, with one side stirring up hurricanes to wreak havoc on the other. But warfare may become less gory with the development of nonlethal gases, and with battles fought 20,000 feet under the sea or between unmanned satellites in outer space.

J. Robert Moskin
"Year 2018"

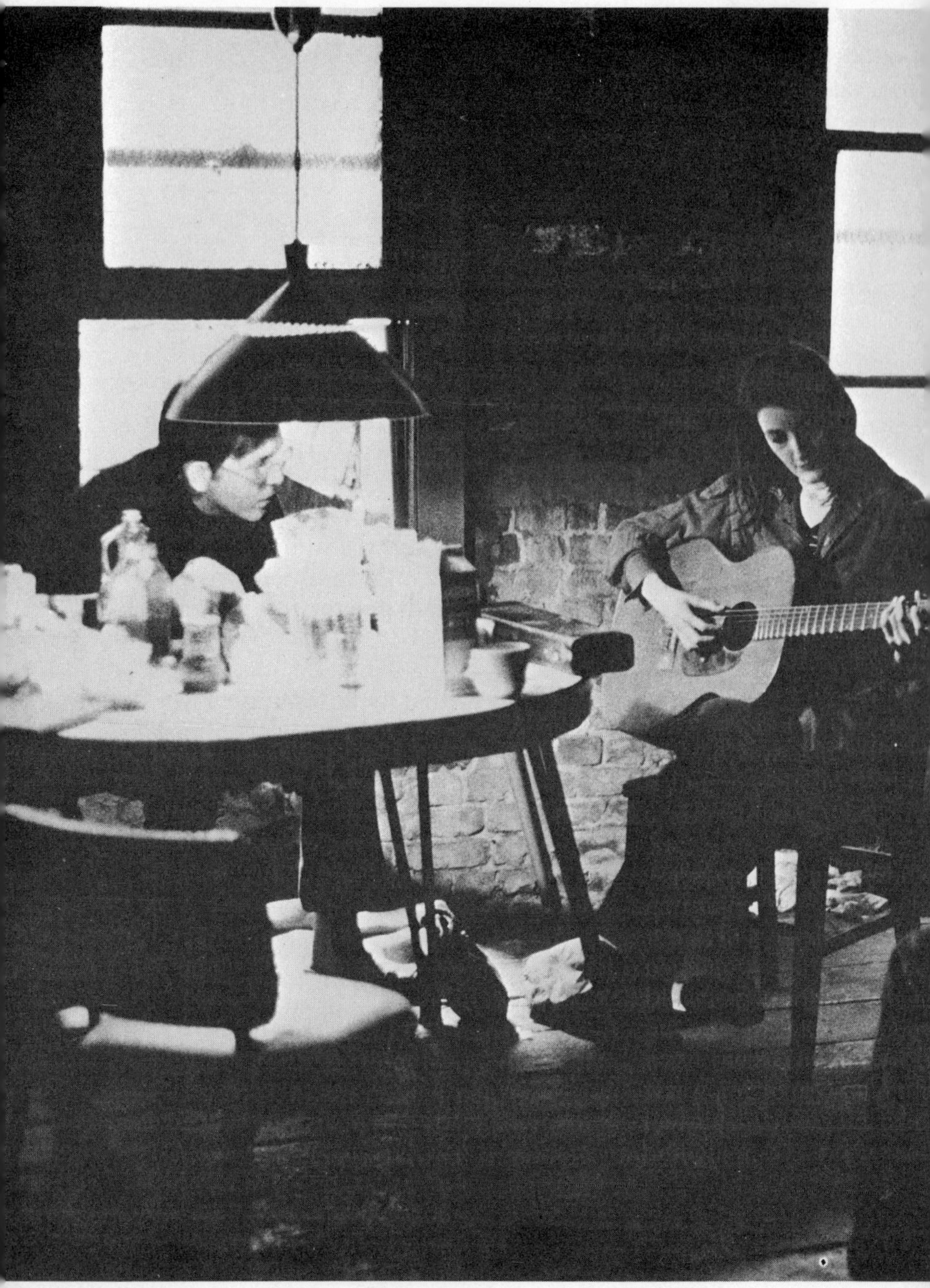

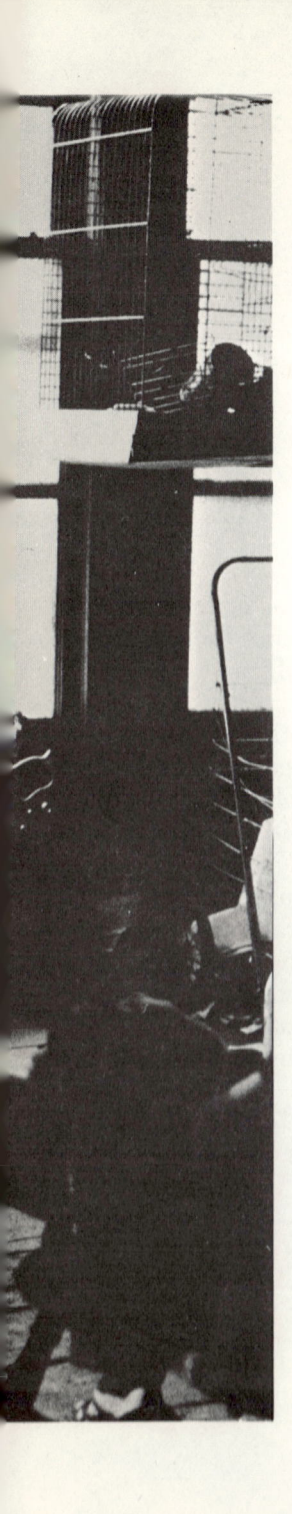

Care as the antidote

Care is important
because it is missing in our day.
What young people are fighting,
in revolts on college campuses
and in the sweep of protests
about the country,
is the seeping, creeping conviction
that nothing matters;
the prevailing feeling
that one can do nothing.
The threat is apathy, uninvolvement,
the grasping for external stimulants.
Care is a necessary antidote for this.

Rollo May

And deep respect

The world is too small
for anything but mutual care
and deep respect;
the world is too great
for anything but responsibility
for one another.

Abraham J. Heschel

Bargaining and compromise

The idea of bargaining may seem prosaic when matched against some of the great ideals and utopias of human aspirations. Yet it is this very principle which is the foundation of a continuing civil society...

The ethic of ultimate ends is, at best, an ethic of conscience. It is an absolute ethic which insists, unconditionally, that the end is so crucial or justifiable that all means necessary may be taken to achieve it, and that no compromise is possible...

The ethic of responsibility is the ethic of compromise. It asks not who is morally right and who morally wrong, but given the potential conflict, how can one solve the problem with least damage for all concerned? With its concentration on civil peace, however, the corruption of this ethic is the loss of principle, or opportunism, into which endless compromise can lead...

The political man, if he is to achieve the "calling" of politics, is aware of both risks, and he knows, in his own maturity, that no single formula or answer will suffice. His only guide is a sense of responsibility—a commitment to his own principles, and a sensitivity to those of others...

Daniel Bell

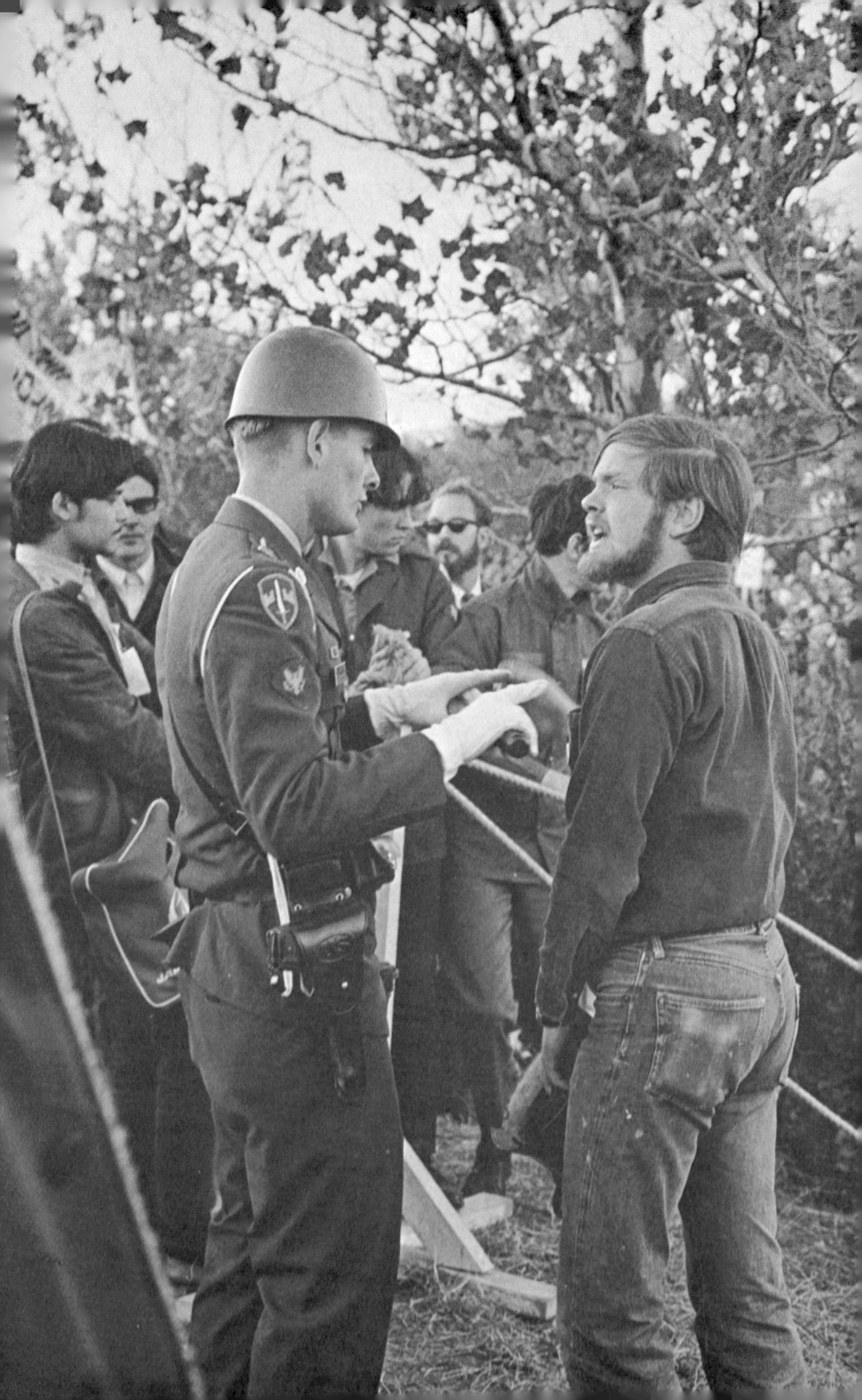

9

THE OTHER PERSON

The secret of this new world and of the new consciousness in the striving for peace is the person. Each person has value both as an individual and as part of the whole. To value the life of all men we must value the life of one man. If a single person had to be tortured or even silenced to achieve a new world, would the new world be worth it? Every sincere expression of thought or opinion adds richness to the fullness of truth.

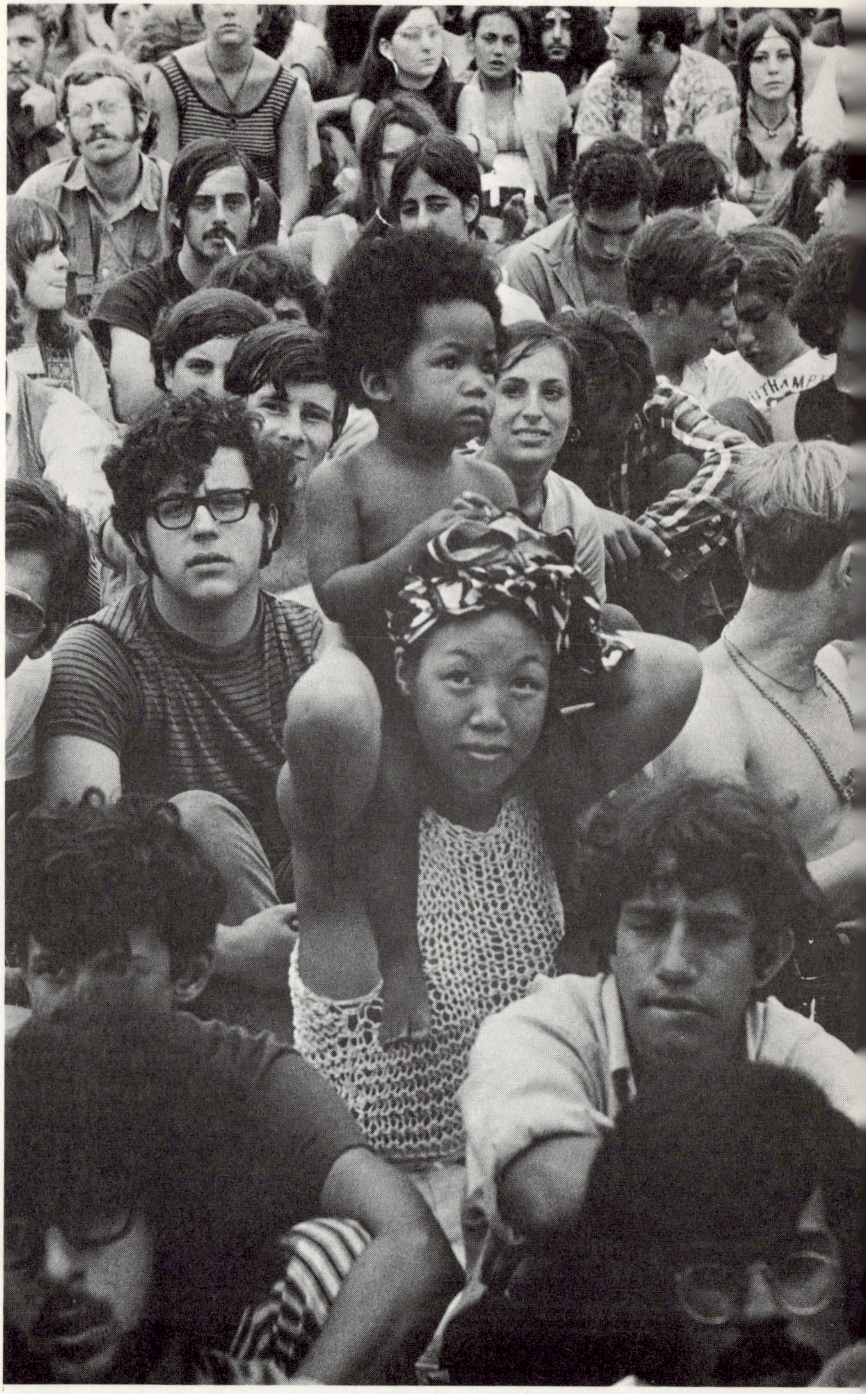

One species

I think I know
what is bothering the students.
What we are up against
is a generation that
is by no means sure it has a future.
The thought that Americans
are in competition
with Russians or with Chinese
is all a mistake, and trivial.
We are one species,
with a world to win.
In the whole universe,
we are the only men.

    George Wald

We are cut in two.
For me, a border clash
is a clash within me.

    Arab storekeeper in Nazareth

War will exist until that day
when the conscientious objector enjoys
the same reputation and prestige
that the warrior does today.

    John F. Kennedy

Only one tiny creature

One can hardly live in rebellion, and I want to live. Tell me yourself, I challenge you—answer. Imagine that you are creating a fabric of human destiny with the object of making men happy in the end, giving them peace and rest at last. Imagine that you are doing this but that it is essential and inevitable to torture to death only one tiny creature—that child beating its breast with its fist, for instance—in order to found that edifice on its unavenged tears. Would you consent to be the architect on those conditions? Tell me. Tell me the truth.

Dostoyevsky
The Brothers Karamazov

The other man

But "the other man," my God—
by which I do not mean
"the poor, the halt, the lame, and the sick,"
but "the other" quite simply as "other,"
the one who seems to exist
independently of me
because his universe seems closed to mine,
and who seems to shatter
the unity and the silence of the world for me—
would I be sincere if I did not confess
that my instinctive reaction
is to rebuff him,
and that the mere thought of entering
into spiritual communication with him
disgusts me?

Pierre Teilhard de Chardin

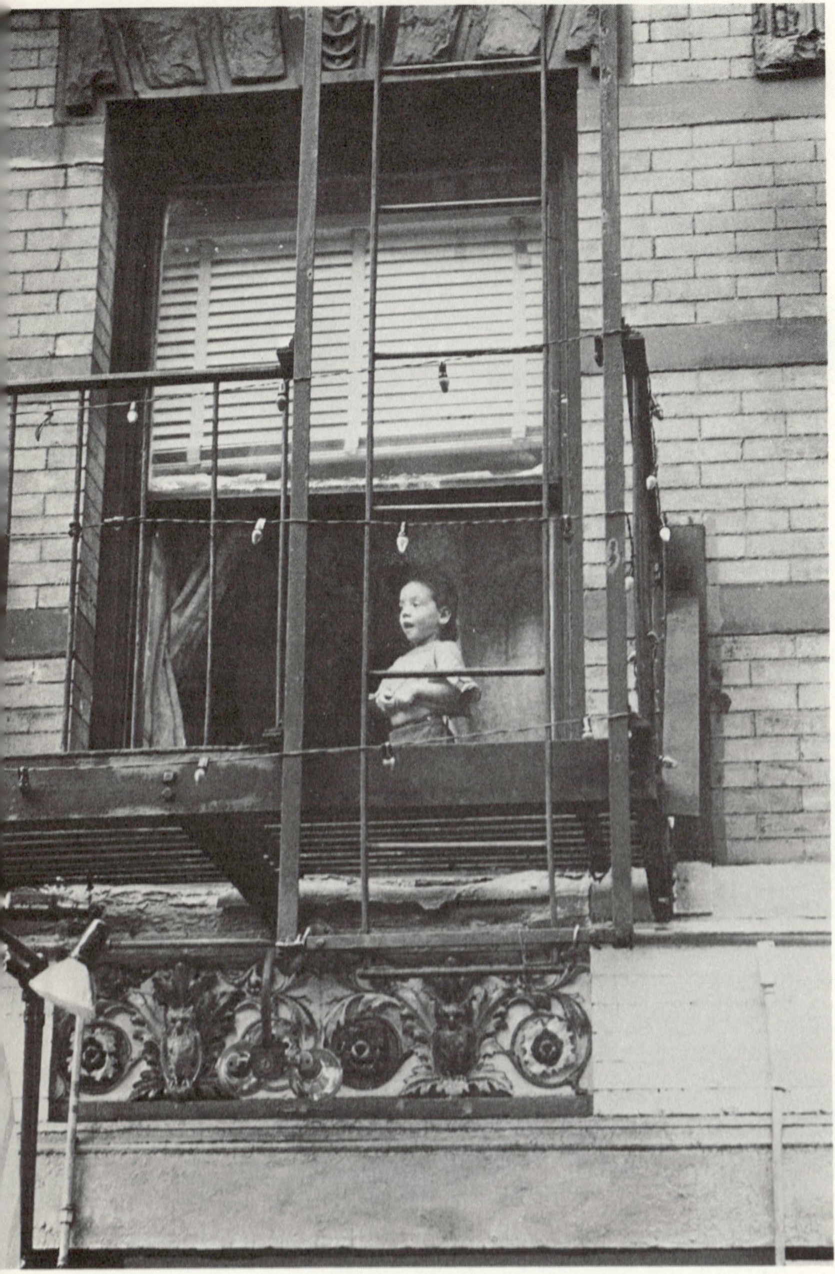

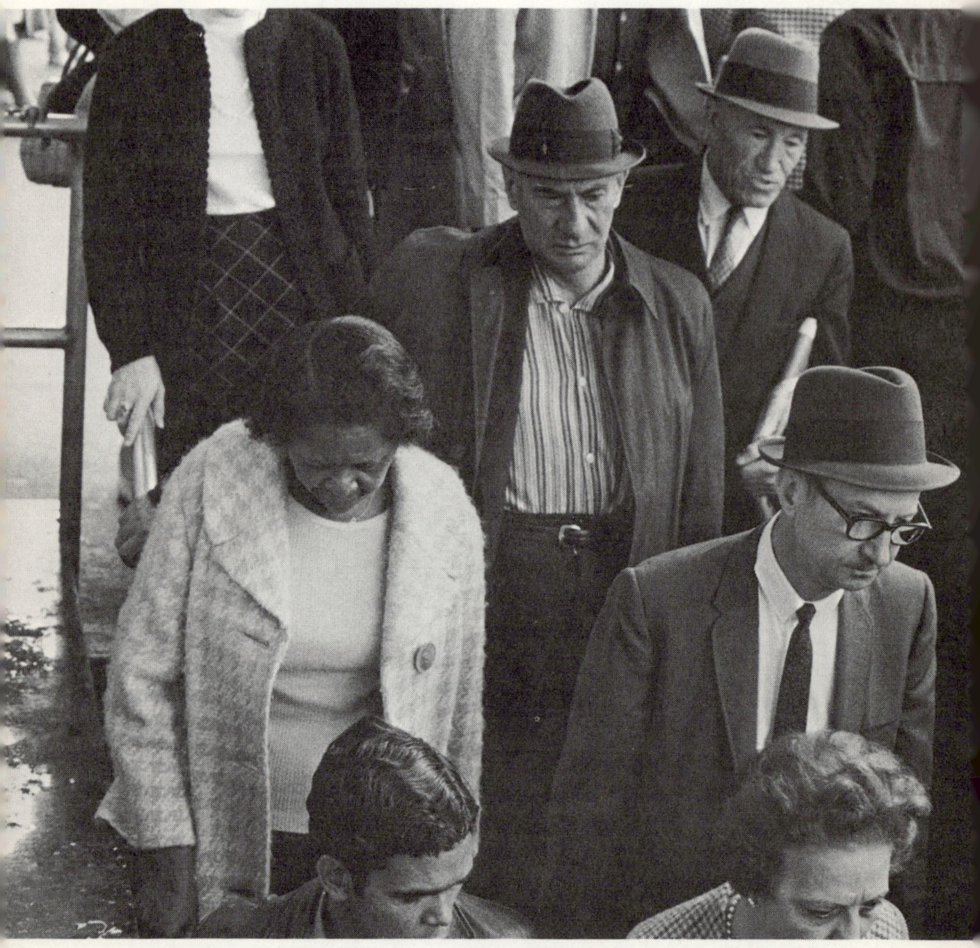

Opinion

If all mankind minus one
were of one opinion,
and only one person
were of the contrary,
mankind would be no more justified
in silencing that one person,
than he, if he had the power,
would be justified
in silencing mankind. . . .
The peculiar evil of silencing
the expression of an opinion
is, that it is robbing the human race;
posterity
as well as the existing generation,
those who dissent from the opinion,
still more than those who hold it.
If the opinion is right,
they are deprived of the opportunity
of exchanging error for truth;
if wrong, they lose,
what is almost as great a benefit,
the clearer perception
and livelier impression of truth,
produced by its collision
with error.

John Stuart Mill
(*On Liberty*, 1859)

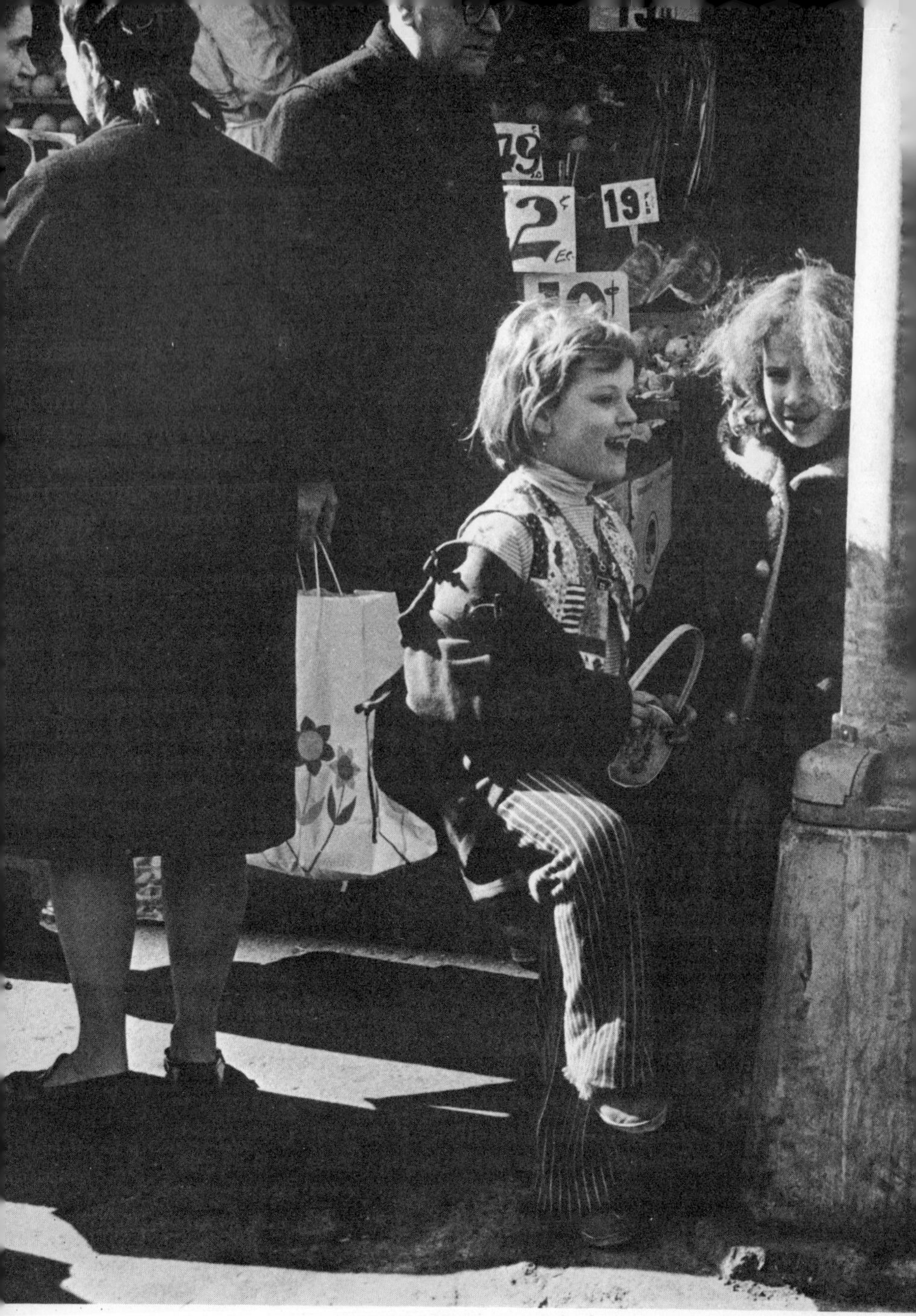
19¢

The great whole

Today is your day and mine,
the only day we have,
the day in which we play our part.
What our part may signify
in the great whole,
we may not understand,
but we are here to play it,
and now is our time.
This we know,
it is a part of action,
not of whining.
It is a part of love,
not cynicism.
It is for us to express love
in terms of human helpfulness.
This we know, for we have learned
from sad experience
that any other course of life
leads toward weakness and misery.

David Starr Jordan

In the Name of God,
the Beneficent,
the Merciful...
whoso saveth the life
of one,
it shall be
as if he had saved
the life of all mankind.

The Koran, Surah V. 32

10

THE FUTURE

At this point in human history mankind can decide how they shall shape their future. Men and women can choose life or destruction; they can put an end to war or create new weapons. They are not powerless to change the direction of things. They are capable of resolving the almost insurmountable difficulties in finding means to create a peaceful future.

Tomorrow's blueprint is not yet designed: We can hasten the pace of war or turn toward peace and learn to love and rediscover our earth. The choice is . . . ours.

Choose life

I call heaven and earth
to witness against you this day,
that I have set before you
life and death,
blessing and curse;
therefore choose life,
that you and your descendants may live.

                        Deuteronomy 30:19

More than an end to war,
we want an end
to the beginnings of all wars.

            Franklin D. Roosevelt

The world cannot continue
to wage war like physical giants
and to seek peace
like intellectual pygmies.

Basil O'Connor

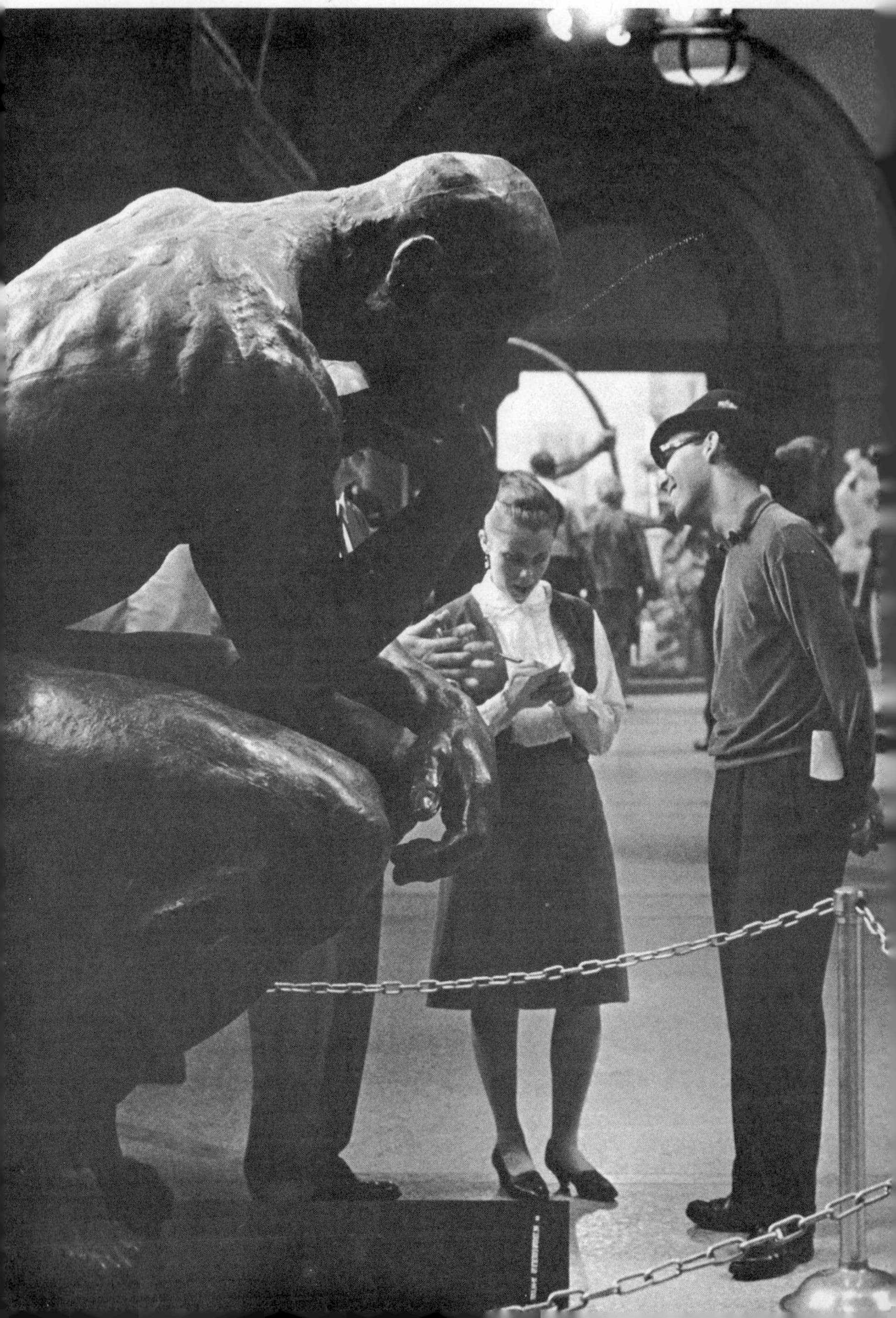

What man has made

Wars are not "acts of God."
They are caused by man,
by man-made institutions,
by the way in which man
has organized his society.
What man has made,
man can change.

      Fred M. Vinson

I decline to accept the end of man.

      William Faulkner

Beyond politics

There is a politic beyond politics
which is concerned with the freedom
of man's mind and spirit.
It looks beyond communism or capitalism
to the welfare of the human family.
Whoever builds upon this politic
will serve humanity
and, in serving, gain its allegiance.

> Bradford Smith

Victory and defeat

Every victory begets hate,
because the one you overcome is not blessed.
Only the one who forgoes
both victory and defeat,
content and glad at heart, is truly blessed.

> Buddha

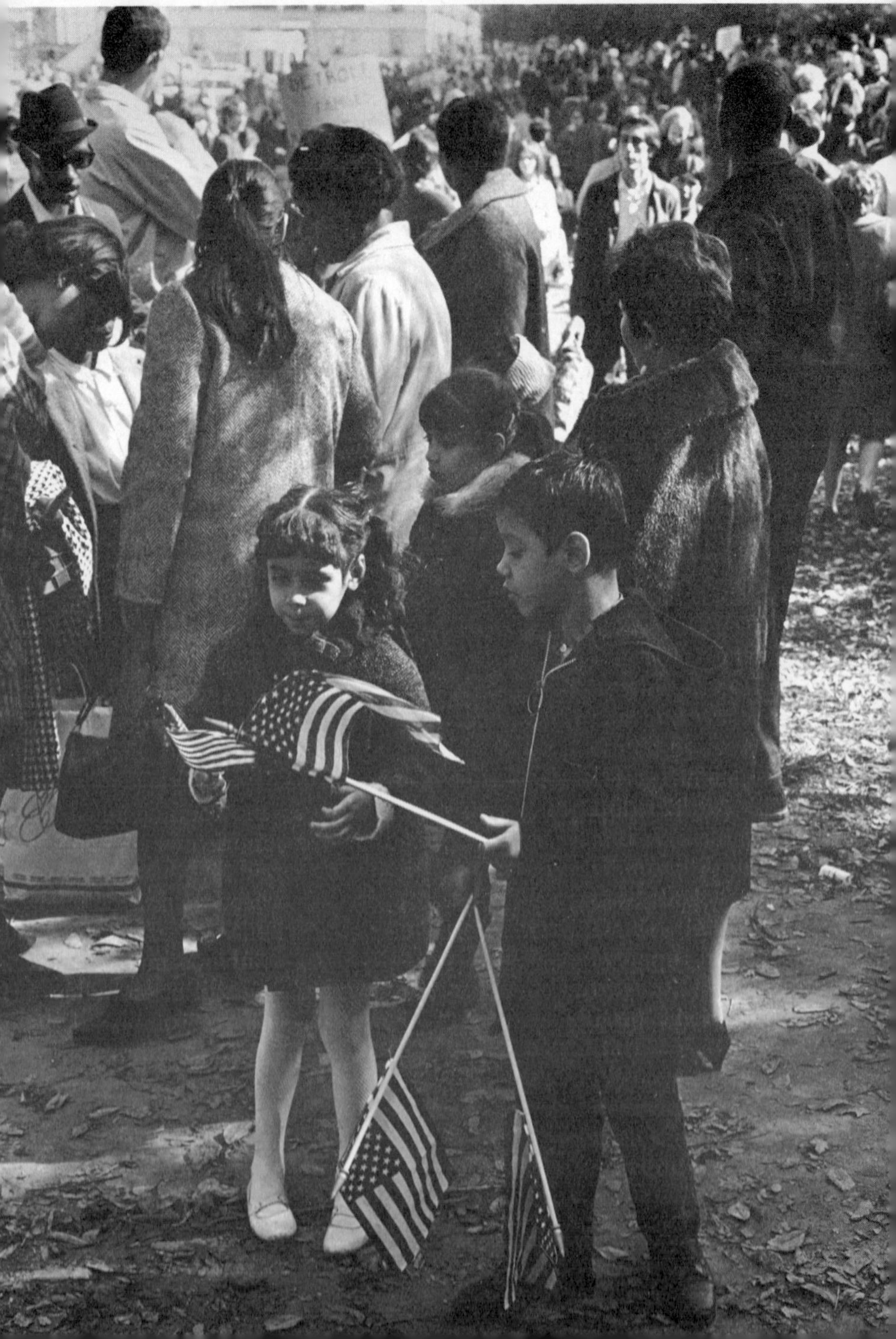

What might be out there

There is risk in it.
There are no maps.
No one has ever been there.
Yet we can make out footprints
all around us, each one
made by someone unique,
none of them made by a person
who is a Xerox copy
of someone else.

It is not a goal that intrigues us,
but a dimension, not a fail-safe
A-to-B-to-C procedure
for arriving at some static point
but the possibility of a glimpse,
even if it is blurred,
of what might be out there.
It is the future.
And its risks are banished
by its relevance
and its fascination.

      Mason Williams

There must be, somewhere,
such a rank as Man.

      Alexander Pope

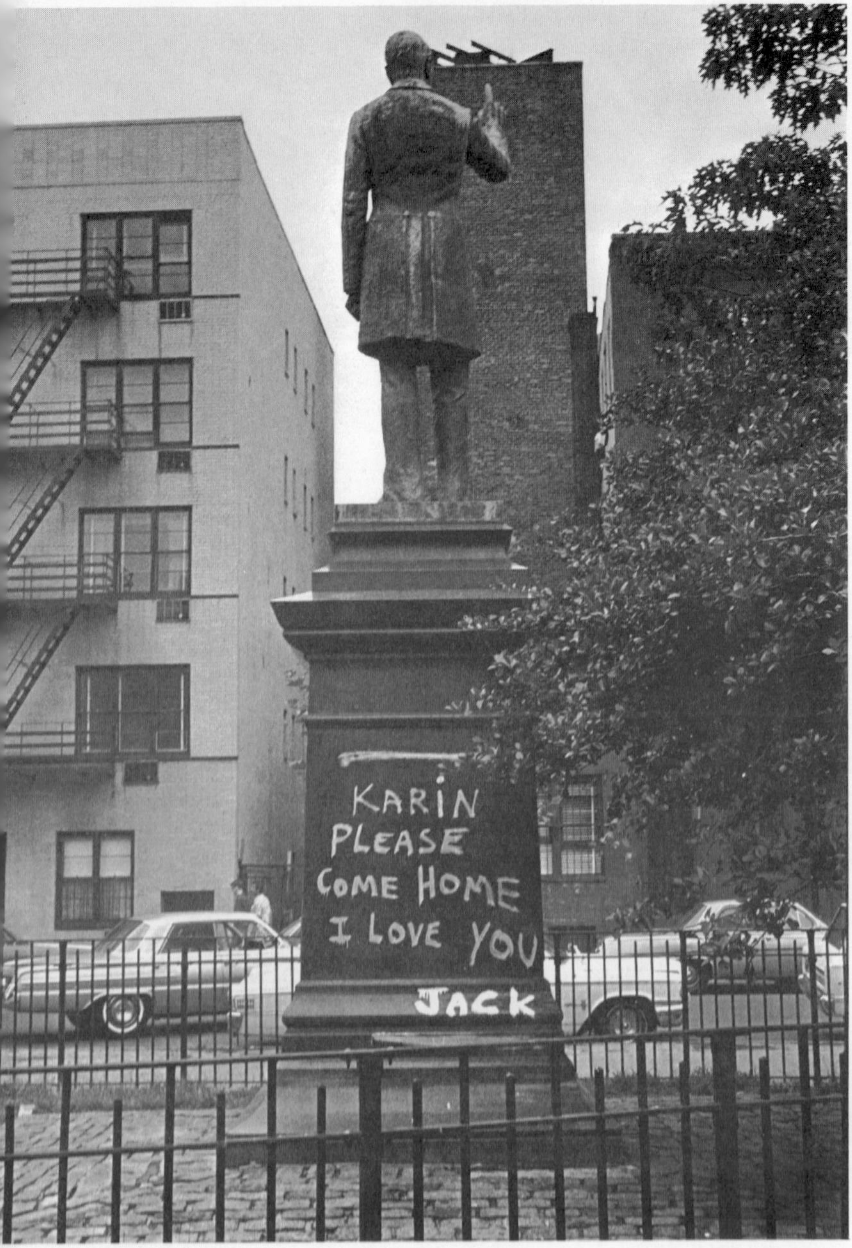
KARIN
PLEASE
COME HOME
I LOVE YOU
JACK

A fantasy

Start by rediscovering
the forgotten earth.
Reality often shows its truest,
strongest colors
through fantasy
so step back from man's troubles
and refresh your courage
with an exercise in imagination.
Be a visitor,
with a little girl and her brother,
on a foreign planet.
See it with clean eyes.
The girl runs across
its glowing shoulder,
wondering if the warm hulk under her
is alive.
Never sure
of what she will find,
she calls to her brother
and sets out to roam
past those dark hills below.

                            John Poppy

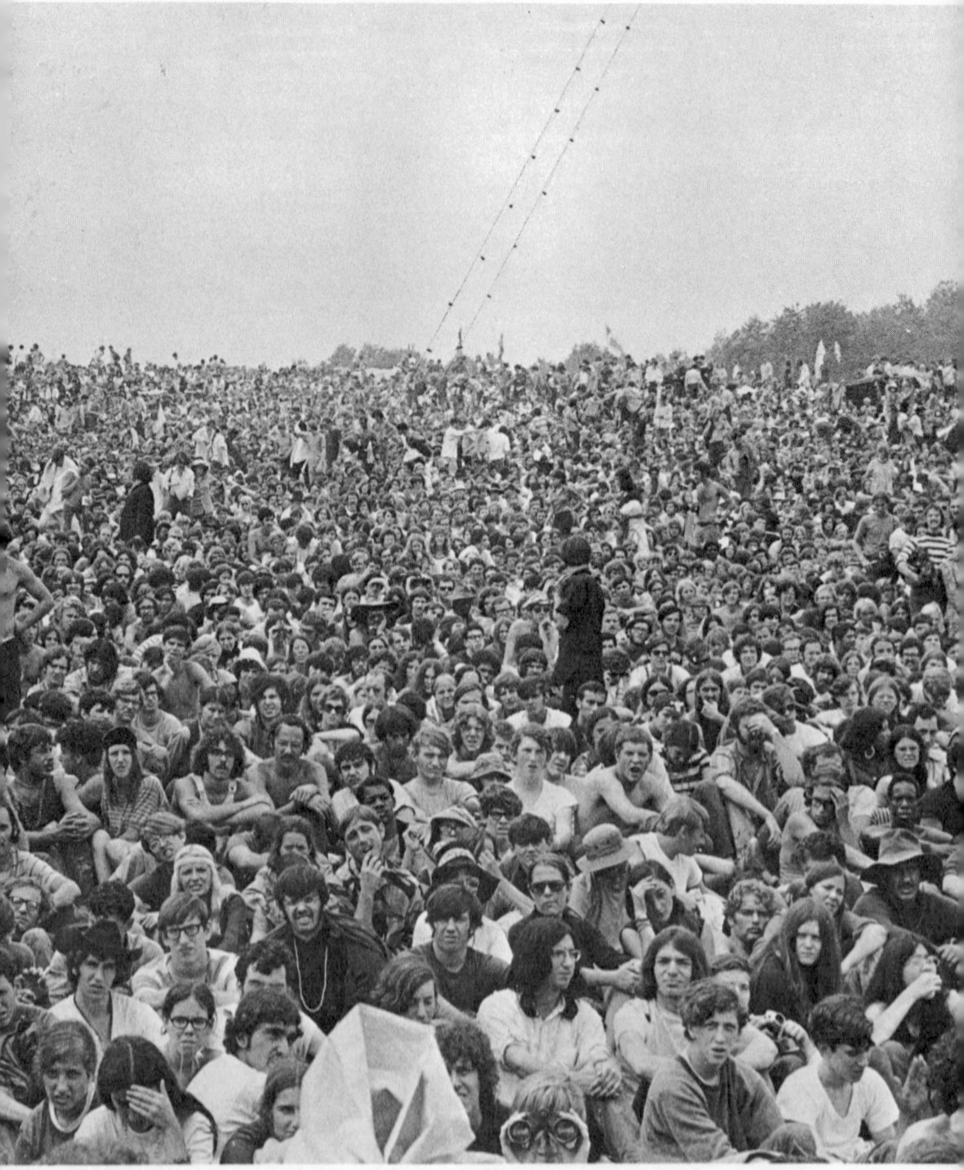